What people are

The Saviour Fish

Mark Weston's book is a delight. From charming neighbourhood children to failing fish stocks, not forgetting the perfect recipe for banana beer, *The Saviour Fish* is a compelling account of life on a remote Tanzanian island, told by a writer who has his eyes wide open and his heart fully engaged.
James Copnall, Presenter, Newsday, BBC World Service, and author of *A Poisonous Thorn in Our Hearts: Sudan and South Sudan's Bitter and Incomplete Divorce*

Weston takes us with him on a remarkable journey, punctuated by well-drawn anecdotes and sharp observations, and brought to life by his elegant description. *The Saviour Fish* is a charming, compelling exploration of Lake Victoria and its people.
Simon Allison, *Mail & Guardian*

Weston's account of the disappearance of Lake Victoria's fish is both alarming and absorbing. *The Saviour Fish* is a wake-up call for the world as it burns through its biodiversity.
David Steven, UN Foundation

An engaging story, bustling with the vibrancy of rural Tanzania and the economic, social, and ecological challenges that are shaping life on the island.
Nathan Hayes, Economist Intelligence Unit

Other Books by this Author

The Ringtone and the Drum: Travels in the World's
Poorest Countries
978 1 78099 586 1

African Beauty
978 1 79709 491 5

The Saviour Fish

Life and Death on Africa's Greatest Lake

The Saviour Fish

Life and Death on Africa's Greatest Lake

Mark Weston

EARTH
BOOKS

Winchester, UK
Washington, USA

JOHN HUNT PUBLISHING

First published by Earth Books, 2022
Earth Books is an imprint of John Hunt Publishing Ltd., No. 3 East St., Alresford,
Hampshire SO24 9EE, UK
office@jhpbooks.com
www.johnhuntpublishing.com

For distributor details and how to order please visit the 'Ordering' section on our website.

Text copyright: Mark Weston 2021

ISBN: 978 1 78904 858 2
978 1 78904 859 9 (ebook)
Library of Congress Control Number: 2021930349

A CIP catalogue record for this book is available from the British Library.

Design: Stuart Davies

UK: Printed and bound by CPI Group (UK) Ltd, Croydon, CR0 4YY
Printed in North America by CPI GPS partners

We operate a distinctive and ethical publishing philosophy in
all areas of our business, from our global network of authors to
production and worldwide distribution.

Contents

For if one link in nature's chain might be lost, another and another might be lost, until this whole system of things will evanish by piecemeal.

Thomas Jefferson

One

On the jetty, a tongue of ochre earth sliding gently into the lake, two women in brightly coloured calico dresses are arguing with a vendor of used clothes. The women have bought T-shirts – European castoffs that have made their way into the African black economy – but the vendor, a bony-faced man in a grubby white baseball cap, has no change. He has asked them to wait while he goes off to ask another hawker to help out, but the women, fearing that he will abscond with their money, have demanded that he leave each of them an additional T-shirt as a guarantee. 'I can't do that,' the man pleads. 'How do I know you won't run off with them when the gate opens?'

'Run off with them?' one of the women shouts, her brow glistening with sweat. 'Do you take us for thieves?'

'No,' says the man. 'But what will you do if it opens while I'm away?'

'We will wait here. When you come back with the change, we will give you back the other two shirts.'

A crowd has coalesced to watch. The women, chests puffed out, grip their purchases. The T-shirt seller does not move. Porters running towards the boat with sacks on their backs pause to take in the spectacle. Other hawkers peer over shoulders to find out why nobody is interested in their wares. From the tin roof of the ticket office, black-winged marabou storks peer down, perhaps wondering if the kerfuffle will leave them any useful debris. The midday sun pummels the shadowless throng.

Finally, a man in a grey shirt and pressed trousers tires of the quarrel and pushes his way to the front of the audience. 'I'll change the money,' he says gruffly, proffering a few furry notes. The vendor, humbled, gives him the two larger notes and hands the still-grumbling women their change. The excitement over, the crowd turns back to the original target of its attention: us.

I am standing with my wife Ebru at the Nyehunge port in Mwanza, Tanzania's second-largest city. The port has an official name, but everybody knows it after the *MV Nyehunge*, the orange and white ferry that waits for us at the foot of the ramp, slowly filling with crates of beer, boxes of cooking oil and sacks of sugar carried on porters' heads or backs.

After a pre-dawn rise in the coastal city of Dar es Salaam, we had missed the morning ferry while we waited at Mwanza's airport for our luggage. The hold of our plane, we discovered after most of our fellow travellers had collected their bags from the belt, had been deemed by the Precision Air Company to be too full to accommodate every passenger's luggage, and the decision had been taken to dispatch it on a later flight instead. Other unfortunates complained to the airline representative; knowing from experience that this would be futile, Ebru and I took our hand luggage outside and sat on trolleys in the shade of the arrivals hall.

In Dar es Salaam, people had told us that Mwanza airport was riddled with thieves. We stayed close to our bags, moving only when the rising equatorial sun shunted us closer to the building. Ebru would tell me later that she had hoped we would miss the afternoon ferry as well, which would have given us one more night on the mainland. I too had felt apprehensive, but the view of the south-eastern corner of the lake we had been given when our plane banked to take a turn before landing had fortified me – green fields flecked with grey rocks, a strand of pale beach, the vast, darkly rippling surface. When our luggage arrived only four hours later than scheduled, I was on balance pleased as well as surprised.

Now we were waiting again, for the gate in the wire fence to open. The ferry's departure time was long past. Mary, the young woman from Dar who had been sent to accompany us, said that in the provinces such delays were the norm (although Mwanza is one of Africa's fastest-growing cities, it is regarded by coast-dwellers as bush). She herself had given us a minor scare that morning when arriving at the airport only just in time for our flight. Seeing that she was taking a long time to get ready – dressing up, as is the Tanzanian way, for the journey – her father had told her to hurry. 'They will be waiting for you,' he said. 'These people keep time. They are different from us.' He had called her while she was in the taxi. We had called her too, to find out where she was. 'You see?' her father said when she told him of our concern. 'I warned you.'

Mary has never seen the lake before. As the other passengers' stares bear down on us – on Ebru and me but also on Mary with her light skin, tight blue jeans and expensive plaited hair extensions – she too looks uneasy, anxious for the gate to open to relieve the pressure. The crowd is thickening – women in patterned dresses or wraparound skirts, men in untucked shirts and T-shirts, sleeping babies swaddled around the backs of teenage girls. Among the legs weave barefoot street children, searching for pockets to pick. We gather closer to our feet the baggage that will keep us for the next two years. Passing hawkers make jokes about us, some in Swahili, others in Kisukuma or Kikerewe, languages of the lake with which Mary is unfamiliar. They offer us socks, boxes of soap, plastic crucifixes and sliced white bread. As we wait in the midday heat, our sweat dripping onto our bags, Mary stands by us like a museum guard.

At length the gate is opened. It is wide enough for only one person to squeeze through. The hundreds waiting outside it surge forward, boxes and battered suitcases borne on heads, buckets and plastic bags dangling in a thicket of legs. There are smells of fish and sweat. Brows glisten under headscarves and baseball caps. Shouts and laughter jostle in the hot air as the teeming horde presses on the sagging fence.

Mary is keen to board. With our seventy kilos of luggage

contained in two rucksacks, four plastic storage bags, two holdalls and a bucket-sized aluminium water filter that has broken during the journey and will spend the coming months as a rubbish bin, Ebru and I think it best to wait until the crush has abated. A porter with an empty trolley promises relief, but since he will reach the deck before us and through a different gap in the fence, Mary fears that if we take up his offer it will be the last we see of our belongings. On the ramp that slants down from the front of the ferry, a white truck with the words SAMAKI TU – Just Fish – stencilled on its sides is reversing in beside another whose windscreen sticker reminds us of God's love. A group of foot passengers shuffling between the two vehicles is almost felled by the manoeuvre.

The ferry's horn honks cheerily. We lift our loads and edge towards the gate. Ahead of us in the melee a young mother with a child at each knee causes a momentary pile-up when she stops to rummage in the folds of her skirt for her tickets. After passing through the gate, our tickets clipped, we exhale as the path opens up towards the waiting vessel. The crowd surges up the vehicle ramp and onto the lower deck between the trucks. Boxes and metal poles are scattered around the puddled floor. Around the back of the vehicles, outside the third-class lounge which is already spewing out surplus passengers, a single vertical ladder climbs to a second deck. Women with buckets on their heads ascend it gingerly. Young men ignore it and leap up using railings and piles of sacks as springboards. At the foot of the ladder another pile-up accretes, as the laden scores wait to climb.

When our turn comes, Ebru and Mary clamber up first. My load is the heaviest and, fettered by a bulging rucksack on each shoulder, it takes all my strength to ascend. There is shouting behind me, and pushing from all sides as I strain upwards. Unburdened youths rise lightly past as if on wings. The sun wrings me out like a sponge. I pause halfway to gather strength, but the strength doesn't come and laughter infiltrates the shouting. I consider giving up and spending the journey on the wet floor under the trucks, but at that moment an arm reaches down from above – brown, smooth skin, plump female fingers. I look up. A plaited-haired young woman bent at the waist smiles down kindly. In one hand she has two plastic water bottles filled with thick green avocado juice. With the other she grabs the strap of the rucksack at my right shoulder and pulls it upwards. There are more guffaws from below as I allow myself to be hauled up. I step with relief onto the deck, and my guardian angel disappears to hawk her wares.

The second deck is an expanse of grey metal open to the sun. Ebru and Mary leave the bags with me and climb another ladder at the rear to look for our seats in the second-class lounge. There is no first-class, and the man in the ticket office, seeing the colour of our skin, had sold us second- rather than third-class tickets without asking our preference. The tickets turn out to be of no relevance – our seats are occupied, their inhabitants unwilling to budge. This news comes as a relief, since none of us is eager for another heavily laden climb. Passengers course onto the deck through the gap in the railings at the top of the ladder. They fan out, each finding a niche. Some slouch against the railings at the front, some on boxes or sacks, others recline behind the ladder leading up to second-class. We push our bags to a patch of shade provided by a pile of foam mattresses, and settle down among them on the metal floor.

Again we wait, sweat drying on our skin, wondering why we let ourselves in for these things. An hour and a half after the ferry's scheduled departure time there is another blast of the horn and the engine rumbles into life. New arrivals continue to pour through the gap in the railings. A number of passengers are already asleep, sprawling on one another's shoulders, backs or laps. Hawkers touting newspapers and sweets pick their way among the prone bodies. Neither their movements nor their negotiations are hurried – the firing up of the engine doesn't appear to signal imminent departure.

A little over half an hour later, the sun's descent by now quite advanced, the ferry moves off. We ease astern, the bow end of the hull scraping the rock-studded slope of the slipway. A trail of thick black smoke hangs in the still air above us as we churn backwards through the frothing lake water. After reversing for three hundred yards the engine noise cranks to a roar and the boat comes to a halt. For a moment I wonder if we have broken down, but then we begin to move forward again, back towards the jetty. As we near it the vehicle ramp, which has been slowly rising into place for the journey, is lowered, and a pair of relieved latecomers leap on board. We reverse again, before this time turning heavily northwards. We are finally under way.

Our progress is stately. A cyclist pedalling along a lakeside path keeps pace with us for a while before disappearing behind trees. As we putter out into the vast expanse of open water the mattresses' shade slips elsewhere, leaving us exposed to the sun's glare. The other passengers, these people who will be our neighbours for the next two years, stare at us, many vacantly, a few with more intensity. The bare feet of those sitting atop the pile of mattresses swing between our heads. I take out a bottle of sun cream and lather it on my forearms and shins. A man sitting near us makes a comment. Others laugh in response. A deck-wide conversation about our motives ensues, not all of it translated by Mary.

'They must want something from us,' says one.

'They must see potential there,' says another.

'They never leave empty-handed.' A round of knowing nods in response.

Mary makes forced conversation. She takes a picture with her phone of the three of us huddled among the dangling feet – to show her father, she says. A man in a vest thinks she is photographing those sitting beyond her outstretched arm. 'Be civilised,' he spits. When she tries to explain herself he gives her a sceptical look and continues talking to his neighbours. Mary turns back to us, chastened.

I try to comfort her by suggesting that it's natural for them to ask why we are here, and natural for them to be suspicious. We are the only white people on the boat, obviously far from home and new to the country. We are accompanied by a smartly dressed bilingual chaperone from the coast. And we are carrying enough luggage for a long haul to a place that is little known to the rest of Tanzania, much less to the outside world. In their shoes, I told her, I would have been interested too.

Mary was not inclined to assuage their curiosity. We were here – or rather, Ebru and Mary were here – as part of a British government aid project that aimed to help modernise teaching methods and improve the level of English in Tanzanian schools. Each of the country's three dozen teacher training colleges was to receive a trainer with expertise in teaching English as a foreign language. Many colleges were in remote parts of the country, a legacy of the independence leader Julius Nyerere's efforts to unite his new nation by scattering public sector workers far from their home regions. Tanzania's dearth of English speakers was a hangover from that same impetus – Nyerere had chosen Swahili rather than the language of the former colonial power as the lingua franca and the language of instruction in schools. Compared with their neighbours in Kenya, Zambia and Uganda, Tanzanians spoke excellent Swahili, but floundered in English.

The college to which Ebru had been assigned was among the farthest-flung. She was late to the project and by the time she signed up the most popular locations – those in cities, and in particular those near Dar es Salaam – had already been taken. She was initially given a choice of three schools, one of which was in the largest town in western Tanzania and another near the capital, Dodoma. Ebru had told her new employers that either of these would be fine, but a few days later she was informed that her three options had been whittled down to one. 'How do you feel about spending two years on an island in a lake?' read the message I received from her while driving with my septuagenarian mother along a country lane on a summer afternoon in Dorset. I gulped, but my nervousness was mixed with excitement. Ebru said she felt sick. My mother kept her thoughts to herself.

But with the contract already signed we had no choice. We knew, moreover, that the project would be interesting for Ebru to work on and potentially useful for her students. I, meanwhile, had nothing better to do, and having spent a good deal of time in urban Africa thought it would be an opportunity to learn something of rural life. Within three weeks of finding out about the posting we had moved out of our rented flat in Spain, deposited possessions in the garages of various friends, stuffed our bags with hot-weather clothes, medical supplies and books, and boarded a plane to East Africa.

The passengers' analysis of our intentions eventually runs its course, and their conversation moves on to the subject of our glacial progress across the lake. The reason for the ferry's sluggishness, it turns out, is the reluctance of the businessman who owns it to spend more than the bare minimum on fuel. There is another ferry, the British-built *MV Clarias*, which departs from a different dock in Mwanza in the mornings and is run by the government. That boat is half a century old and has a maximum speed of some five knots. The privately owned ferries that are in competition with it – this one and the one we had missed that morning – therefore have no need to hurry. They save fuel by travelling at half their maximum speed, still arrive before the *Clarias*, and a journey that could be completed in two hours seldom takes less than four.

I stand to stretch and look at the lake. Lake Victoria – Africa's largest lake, the world's second largest. Abode of crocodile, hippopotamus and malaria-bearing mosquito. Elusive goal of backstabbing European explorers, the least heralded of whom won the centuries-long race to confirm it as the source of the Nile and named it after his queen. An inland sea the size, roughly, of Ireland, and a life source, today, for millions.

The lake is silvery in the afternoon sunlight. To the west, the low hills of the mainland slide into still, open water that stretches as far as the eye can see. To the east, green hills topped by rampart-like grey boulders march off into the distance. The boulders, the size of apartment blocks, are the sequelae of ancient, continent-sundering convulsions. In their lee squat tiny single-storey houses, their tin roofs glinting in the sun. As I look at these houses, dwarfed by the great granite towers behind them, it occurs to me in my slightly enervated mood that it would only take one more Hadean belch to send most of the rocks tumbling into the abyss, driving the crumpling houses like demonised swine before them.

We pass a rocky islet painted white by guano. Near it float two wooden pirogues, paddles resting along their sides. Their crews are invisible, probably asleep. A pelican bobs on the surface of the water, its long bill held stiffly above the smooth-crested wavelets. Ebru and Mary sit chatting at my feet. Behind my head at the top of the ladder to second-class, a seated woman vomits quietly into the gathered-up folds of her flower-patterned skirt.

I look ahead, over the trucks and the raised vehicle ramp. On the northern horizon I make out a long grey smudge, floating in the haze above the lighter grey of the lake. At first I take it for cloud, but it could, I realise with an anxious pang, be land. The ferry ploughs on, the drone of the engine muffling the cries of the few gulls that have continued to follow us. The sun is lower in the sky now and the intensity has gone from its heat. A few other passengers have risen to their feet and are leaning on the side panels or the railings above the trucks, also staring ahead. Gradually the shape of the floating line to the north grows clearer, solidifying into a long strip of low grey hills. To either side, where the land trails off into the lake, there is open space, nothingness. Beyond, I know from my reading, this nothingness stretches for hundreds of miles. The smudge is Ukerewe, the lake's largest island – our home, if we can hack it, for the next twenty-four months.

The ferry continues its steady grind. The island looms closer, filling the prospect, its ends no longer in sight. Off to our left, heading in the direction of Mwanza, I spot a small black sail billowing gently in a soft breeze. Held up by two slender tree branches, its lower edge dips in the water. As it turns it glints in the sun, and I see that it is made of something like polythene, no thicker than a bin liner. In the flimsy dugout behind it sit two men, silhouetted by the declining sun.

By now most of the passengers on the deck are standing. They look ahead and chat in low voices. With Mary's help we try to engage the men sitting on the mattress in conversation. We ask them how to greet people in Kikerewe. They tell us in Swahili that the language of the Kerewe people is not the only language spoken on the island; there are also Kijita and Kikara, spoken by the Jita and the Kara people. But they are happy to help us learn, and delighted that we have taken an interest. They watch as I write the greetings in the back of my Swahili textbook – *wanagiramu, wasibamu, tulabonana*. When we try them out they laugh, but now their laughter is friendly rather than scornful. Other passengers gather round to join in.

The sun drops below the island's western hills. Passing a promontory which extends into the lake like a giant crocodile snout, the ferry turns into a horseshoe bay. To our right the scrub-covered hills are darkening from light green to grey. Those to the left are shadowed in indigo. The beaches below the hills are fringed with bushy trees, thick and dark and overhanging. The bay closes in, enfolding us. The air is warm and still. Kites circle above in a darkening steel-blue sky. A leaning dhow, its patched-together sail the shape of a rose thorn, crosses our path on its way out into the lake. Ahead, above a tangle of dark trees, I see a twist of smoke rising, then another further back as preparations begin for the evening meal. Palm tops protrude above the canopy as if keeping watch.

The engine cuts to a purr and the ferry drifts slowly landwards. A whitewashed building close to the shore comes into view in the waning light. Overhung by palms, it stands on a short concrete jetty at the top of a muddy slope. Its firm art deco lines are undermined by curls of peeling paint. It has the look of a customs house or arrivals hall, perhaps Indian, but it appears to be abandoned and we slide instead towards a ramp of flattened earth.

Dusk sweeps in. Beyond the ramp climbs a dirt track, lined at ground level by the glowing candles of crouching market ladies. Behind the women on one side ascends a row of scruffy shacks under collapsing corrugated-iron roofs. Dark figures make their way down the track towards the wire gate. The ferry passengers crowd above the ladder. We hang back by the mattresses, keeping an eye on our bags as passengers from the upper deck stream past. Darkness falls and the boat drifts towards the ramp. The horn sounds twice, its fading caw giving way to the sudden growl of gunned motorcycle engines. A web of headlights pops into life beyond the wire fence as motorbike taxi drivers get ready for their fares. In the faint glow beyond stand waiting hawkers, their trays protruding from their stomachs.

The ferry nudges the tyres chained to the end of the slipway. Passengers flow down the ladder. The bow ramp is lowered, and the exiting travellers are met by an onrush of blue-shirted stevedores who push between the trucks and swing up via the railings to our deck. The men gather sacks and boxes and drop them to colleagues waiting below. Up through the warm air rise the shouts of porters and buffeted passengers. The trucks move off, broad-shouldered porters under bulging sacks lurching in their wake. One of the men spots us at the rear of the deck. With a confident smile he picks up most of our bags as if they were empty. We gather the remainder and follow him down to the vehicle deck.

As we reach dry land and make our way along the ramp towards the wire fence we are intercepted by a small, gaunt-faced man standing by a white jeep. He wears an untucked white shirt and black slacks, and he is polite and a little formal as he asks the porter to put our bags in the boot. He turns to Ebru and introduces himself. 'I am Mr Sahili,' he says in English with a shy smile. 'I am the College Principal.' He shakes our hands and holds the back door open as we climb in. The college driver turns to introduce himself. He is stout and tall, too large for his seat. 'I am Yuve,' he grins. 'Welcome to Ukerewe' (*Ooh-keh-REH-weh*, he pronounces it). We tip the porter through the window, and are driven off into the darkness.

Two

Our first night on the island is spent in a single-storey hotel by the lake. There to welcome us is Gloria, a feisty, strongly built Zimbabwean whom Ebru is to replace at the college. Gloria has been on the island for just three months, but has been granted a transfer to a less remote location. 'There's nothing to do here,' she explains. 'I hope you've brought plenty of films to watch.'

We sit on the steps outside reception, and she lists the other reasons for her premature exit. The unfriendliness of the neighbours, the theft of water from her outside tank, and an attempted break-in while she was asleep one night in her house have combined to make her feel uneasy about being here alone, she says. When an opportunity arose to decamp to the mainland, she jumped at it.

The journey has exhausted me and I am in need of a rest, but Gloria has other ideas. Energised by her imminent departure, she is keen to show us her house, which she tells us is the only place on the island fit for human habitation. After a few minutes resting on the steps, we climb back into Yuve's jeep. He drives us along streets of rutted earth, then along a crumbling paved road that bisects what seems to be a large village. Mr Sahili points to the right and tells us that we are passing the ferry jetty, emptied now of traders. There are no street lamps; the only light comes from little fires in the yards of compounds or through cloths hanging over unglazed windows. Most of the houses – squat rectangular blocks with tin roofs – are cloaked in darkness. It is not yet eight o'clock, but the streets are deserted.

The paved road quickly reverts to dirt, the vehicle shuddering as the surface deteriorates. After a ten-minute ride we pull up outside a house, larger and illuminated a little more brightly than those we have passed. In the thick darkness it appears to be surrounded only by empty bush. We follow Gloria inside and she gives us a tour.

The rooms of the single-storey building are uniform cubes whose walls are decorated by cracks. The ceiling light in the living room gives off a reddish glow that brings to mind a cheap brothel. In a corner between ripped sofas stands a dark-brown refrigerator. In the adjoining dining area, the three chairs at the formica table are broken. One lacks a seat. The two bedrooms lie to the rear of the house, wooden frames draped with torn mosquito nets sprouting from the double beds that are their only furniture. Behind the clear-glass door of the bathroom that abuts the larger bedroom, the toilet is obscured by two tall black plastic containers. There is running water, Gloria tells us, for only an hour every evening, and she keeps the containers full for use in the daytime. The electricity supply, she adds, is fairly reliable, with no more than half a dozen power cuts each week. Ebru seems pleasantly surprised by the house, and Gloria says that looking for something better would be fruitless. In my depleted state, however, the prospect of spending my days here deepens my gloom, and I ask Mary if we can come back in the morning for a second look.

Back at the hotel I leave Ebru, Gloria and Mary chatting on the steps and go inside for a lie-down. Our room is a square box with a white-tiled floor, lit by a single bulb hanging from the ceiling. There is a defunct television on a table in one corner and a dark-cushioned armchair in another. Across the window are drawn red curtains. I switch on the ceiling fan and a shower of dust falls from the blades. As I collapse onto the bed I lack the energy even to kick off my shoes. Just as I'm falling asleep I am called to the empty dining room of the hotel for dinner. The idea of food makes me nauseous, but I manage to keep down a few forkfuls of rice and a couple of strips of the flesh of a large white fish.

That night there is rain. It falls in torrents, stops, then falls in torrents again. There is no build-up, no gradual fade-out. It is as if the rain god has emptied an enormous bucket, then gone off to fetch another.

In the morning we wake early. Refreshed, I open the dust-caked curtains to see a tall grey heron standing in the grassy yard. Nearby, a woman in a wraparound skirt bends at the waist washing tin plates and bowls. The yard is shaded by tall trees, their leaves still wet.

In the dining room we breakfast on sliced white bread, margarine and chunks of papaya fruit. The breakfast materials are laid out on a long trestle table covered by a stained white tablecloth. The kitchen staff are nowhere to be seen. From a flask we pour hot water into dainty porcelain cups, and add *Africafe* coffee from a sachet. In the reception area a young woman in a white blouse is asleep, her arms and head sprawled squid-like over the counter. The hotel seems to have no other guests.

We take our coffees outside and wade down through the damp grass of the hotel's overgrown garden to the lakeside. The lake is smooth and grey under a cloudy sky. We look out over the bay we had entered the previous evening. The hills on the far side appear rockier and more barren in the daylight, those on the near side smoother and grassier. The ferry we came in on has already departed for Mwanza, leaving the slipway vacant. We sit on broken bamboo chairs under a thatched gazebo. A few yards ahead of us in the shallows passes a wooden pirogue paddled by two men in baseball caps. The men stare at us intently. Beyond them a monitor lizard swims in the opposite direction, its brown snout held up like a dog's above the surface.

To either side of the garden, leafy trees harbour egrets and woodland kingfishers. Fifty yards to our left, naked men stand thigh-deep in the lake and lather soap over their gleaming chests and heads. To our right, women do the same, some naked, a few in knickers. Seeing us sitting there alone, one of the men waggles his penis in our direction and shouts. While we pretend not to notice, his friends laugh and slap each other's hands in appreciation of the joke.

From the narrow strand of beach two skinny boys in ragged T-shirts approach us. We fall into conversation in our stilted Swahili. Both aged twelve, Ismail is confident and brash, his friend Joseph reserved and polite. When Ebru asks why they are not at school they giggle, and they giggle again when we refuse their requests to buy them soft drinks. Ismail, short for his age and with a mischievous glint in his narrow eyes, asks me something I don't understand, although I think I hear the letter X. Repeating the question more slowly, he gyrates his hips and makes a smacking motion in front of his groin with his right hand. He is asking me if I like porn films. He loves them, he says. 'You can buy them in the DVD shops.'

When we ask if they study English at school they nod. I ask them to say something. 'Good morning, Madam,' they chorus. Ebru picks up a few sticks and stones from the garden and they gather on the beach for a lesson. The boys stand to attention, each desperate to be the first to answer her questions. Their command of numbers in English is stronger than their greeting abilities, but neither can string a sentence together, and when Ebru asks them to turn her questions back on her – What is this? How many stones? – they dissolve into flummoxed laughter.

Mary calls to us from the road and tells us we have things to do. 'Another tomorrow?' the boys ask in Swahili as we stand to leave. They grin when Ebru assents.

Our first chore is to visit the island's immigration office. On the way we stop near the government ferry jetty to pick up Mr Sahili. The teacher training college lies in the village of Murutunguru in the interior of the island, but as well as being the college principal Mr Sahili has a shop in Nansio that sells liquor and soft drinks, and he has come in to chat to the young man he employs to run it. Many of the teacher trainers would turn out to have similar sidelines, and they would often skip lessons while they attended to business matters.

The paved road leading up from the jetty, Yuve tells us, is the main street of Nansio. The previous night we had taken the place for a village, but Yuve says that it is officially a small town and by far the island's largest settlement. In the early morning there is a little more life on the streets – languid men on bicycles, wandering women with tubs on their heads, shopkeepers laying out their wares, motorbike taxi drivers leaning on their handlebars while they wait for passengers.

The immigration office sits among other council buildings at the top of a small rise on the northern edge of Nansio. The district was established early in the last century by British colonisers. It is leafy and quiet, and its elevation renders it breezier than the sultry town below. Nansio's councillors have their homes here as well as their offices. As a consequence, Yuve tells us with a chuckle, the area has the island's most reliable supplies of electricity and running water. But even in the abode of the powerful, the streets are of rough dirt – only two of the island's roads are paved, our driver reports, and those for a total of less than two miles.

The office is a neat, whitewashed block. Mr Sahili knocks on the door, its blue paint peeling in the heat, and we are called in. The immigration officer, a tall, thin young man in a pressed white shirt, sits behind a wooden desk. Behind him on the wall is a framed photograph of the country's president. On the desk lies a black hardback notebook. There is nothing else – no computer, no telephone, no papers or files, no sign of any work being done or planned. Mr Sahili stands behind us in the doorway as Ebru and I, our knees touching, take seats.

The immigration officer welcomes us in English and tells us his name is Patrick. His tone combines formality with friendliness – his posture is stiff and upright, but his eyes smile along with his thin lips as we tell him what we will be doing here and how long we plan to stay. He is pleased, he says, that we have come to see him so soon after our arrival – Gloria had failed to register, and his assistant had eventually had to stop her in the street. He pushes the notebook towards us and asks us to sign it. A brown goat has joined Mr Sahili at the threshold. Only a few of the pages of the notebook have been used, the names above ours all African. When I ask Patrick why Ukerewe needs an immigration office, he tells me that fishermen come here illegally from the neighbouring lakeshore nations of Kenya and Uganda. Other migrants are on the run from the police, or stopping over on their way to seek work in the gold mines near Mwanza. He confirms that we are the island's only *wazungu*, the unofficial East African word for white people. 'In fact, you are the only ones to have lived here for years,' he says.

This information bolsters the meagre stock of knowledge we have acquired about our new home. Ukerewe seemed reluctant to reveal its secrets, apparently determined to enmesh anyone who showed interest in it in a web of contradiction and confusion. While it was clear, for instance, that ours was the largest island in an archipelago, no two sources agreed how many islands the group comprised. Estimates ranged from twenty-seven to thirty-eight, but many islands seemed to be unnamed, or to have two different names, or to share a name with a neighbour. Distances, too, were muddled. Nansio was somewhere between twenty-two and thirty-four nautical miles from Mwanza. Overland distances could only be guessed at, since Ukerewe remained uncharted even by Google Maps. Estimates of the archipelago's total population, meanwhile – no one was rash enough to hazard a per island figure – began at two hundred thousand and rose to almost half a million.

Other information we had pieced together was murkier still. A guidebook to Tanzania had described the islands as an untouched arcadia, whose inhabitants ate what they grew and were startled by the sight of white people. History books were less effusive. In the 1850s an Arab slaver told the English explorer John Speke that the Kerewe people were hostile and dangerous. Soon after Speke identified the lake as the main source of the Nile, two British missionaries who followed in his wake were murdered on one of the island's beaches after becoming embroiled in a local quarrel. A few years later a group of German evangelists watched their mission burn to the ground as they were driven back to the mainland. Indian traders who came here after the British had ejected the German colonisers from East Africa following World War I met with similar treatment, hounded out by a furious mob after rumours spread that they were defrauding local cotton farmers.

Our limited Swahili made interpreting other sources difficult. A photograph on the internet showed a pile of dead dogs on a jetty. It was accompanied by another of a woman with a bloody gash on one arm, perhaps suggesting the presence of rabies on the island. A number of articles alluded to witchcraft – to human bones ground up and scattered over fishing nets to bring luck, to people with albinism murdered so that their body parts could be used in medicines. One website, by contrast, claimed that Ukerewe was a safe haven for albinos, who had sought sanctuary there after fleeing the witches of the mainland.

Patrick tells us he hopes to leave the island before the year is out. Mr Sahili, who is building himself a house near Mwanza, says that in the past the countries surrounding the lake would deport their criminals here, and that the archipelago is still regarded as a punishment posting for civil servants today. Many of Ebru's students at the teacher training college would tell her that they resented having to live here, not only hundreds of miles from their homes but impossibly far, too, from what they regarded as civilization.

The immigration formalities completed – they extend no further than signing the visitor's book – we are taken to have a second look at the house. In daylight, and with our energy restored, it is transformed. Around it is not empty bush but a neighbourhood of single-room mud-brick houses sheltered by spreading mango trees. Narrow, dusty footpaths weave among the foliage, and colourful clothes hang drying on lines suspended between the branches.

A particularly impressive mango, thick of trunk and bushy of leaf, stands before the black iron grille that encloses our veranda. The house is an apricot-coloured bungalow under a pyramidal corrugated tin roof painted in turquoise. Gloria is away at the teaching college saying goodbye, so a neighbour, a lean-faced man in an untucked black shirt who introduces himself as Dickson, comes over to open the padlocked gate for us. As he fumbles with the keys a posse of children gathers around our legs, looking up and greeting us excitedly. 'Shikamoo,' they say – the respectful Swahili greeting for your elders, whose literal meaning is, 'I clasp your feet.' 'Marahaba,' we reply once, before realising when many of the children repeat their greeting that we are expected to reply to each of them individually. A little boy in a torn T-shirt inserts his hand into mine and stands happily holding it. An equally small girl with plaited hair sees this and grasps Ebru's hand. They chatter among themselves and at Dickson, asking if we are to be the house's new tenants. When he says we are, a few of them jump with glee.

The house is suitable for our needs, and while Ebru is taken to the college to meet her students Mary and I return to the hotel, where she has made an appointment with our new landlord. She leaves me at a lakeside table in the garden while she goes to fetch the rental contract. Bees buzz around the table legs. Clumps of foam ooze from tears in the cushions on my bamboo chair. In the shallows, empty now of naked bathers, black and yellow weaver birds flit between two large bushes.

After some time, two men approach from the direction of the hotel. Both are in their thirties. One of them, of stocky build and with a shaved head and narrow, darting eyes, introduces himself as Mr Masondole. His companion, taller and less confident, is named Renatus. I stand to shake their hands and they take seats on the opposite side of the table.

Gloria has warned us that Masondole, the landlord, is shifty and unresponsive, and that he will swindle us given the chance. We sit in awkward silence, sizing each other up. The sun has yet to elbow aside the morning clouds. Below the tall trees on one side of the garden, a procession of women and girls carrying tubs of clothes and empty jerrycans makes its way to the lake. The two men confer among themselves in a local language, probably Kikerewe. I am beginning to see what Gloria meant, but when I try to break the ice by asking in Swahili whether they speak English their demeanour changes and they pull their chairs closer to the table. Now they seem interested in talking to me, and pleased, like the people on the ferry, that I know a little of their language. It is as if they have been waiting for me to make the first move, even though it is I who am the foreigner here. We talk about football, the great African icebreaker, and Renatus slaps my hand in solidarity when he learns we support the same English team.

Mary walks over to join us, and Masondole asks her to tell me that the problems he had with "Madam Gloria" were the result of a misunderstanding owing to the lack of a common language. He has great respect for Mr Sahili, he adds, and wants us to be happy in the house. When I enquire about the rent, he asks for almost double what Gloria has been paying. He backs down quickly when I tell him we are aware of the going rate (the rate, that is, for foreigners – no islander would give him a tenth of what Ebru's employer was willing to pay). We agree that we will move in five days later, once he has fixed the wire mosquito netting that has come loose on some of the windows. We sign the contract Mary puts before us and shake hands on the deal.

Gloria leaves Ukerewe for good on the afternoon ferry. From the hotel garden we watch as the boat slides away from the jetty and disappears out of the bay. Mary is due to leave two days later – soon we will be alone. That night we meet the hotel's only other guest. A gangling figure with a flat-top, Kwame Nkrumah-style haircut, he has been talking to Mary in the hotel reception area, asking her why we are here. His head is large and heavy-looking, and his shoulders seem too narrow to support such a weight. His forehead bears the first lines of middle-age. He seems to approve of our motives, and when we join them introduces himself in English. 'My name is Vincent,' he says, gazing down at us with a slightly patronising mien, 'but people call me Mabiba.' He smiles, his white teeth contrasting brightly with the dark skin of his face. 'Mabiba means sower of seeds,' he explains, 'and that is what I do.'

He tells us he is a Christian entrepreneur. Born on Ukerewe and brought up Roman Catholic, he moved away from the island at an early age and, after completing his studies at a seminary school in Mwanza, settled in Dar es Salaam. Ukerewe was not always poor, he says, 'as you see it now,' but once had a thriving economy. A few farmers and fishermen grew so wealthy that they were able to build schools to help their fellow islanders. 'We have produced many professors and senior civil servants,' he tells us. 'Even a former Speaker in the National Assembly.'

In Dar es Salaam, and then for a few years in Australia, Mabiba worked in the hotel industry. While overseas he began to read books on spiritual entrepreneurship. Religion had always been an important part of his life, and he saw that this was a path he could follow. When he returned to Dar he became aware of Winners' Chapel International, a megachurch founded in Nigeria in 1981. Winners' embrace of prosperity and success – two of its twelve core tenets – struck a chord with the budding businessman, and when the church's multimillionaire founder appeared before him in a vision and presented him with a book he had authored, he decided to join up.

'It is depressing to see all these people with no hope or confidence,' he says as we sit on sofas in the ill-lit reception, assailed by whining squadrons of mosquitoes. 'Our church says it is good to seek prosperity and to rise up in the world. Other churches say we are too materialistic, but it is our belief that people do not need to live in poverty and without hope. We try to change their mindset. We tell them that if you have faith, determination and patience, everything is possible.'

On Ukerewe the church's anti-poverty message is an enticing one. Mabiba is working for a company that installs pipelines to pump water from the lake to the island's villages, but his passion is the small church he has established in Nansio. A Winners' Chapel pastor comes from Mwanza every week to preach at Sunday mass, while Mabiba himself leads the Wednesday and Friday services. 'The church is on the site of what was once a bar,' he says. 'But there was a problem with demonic slapping.' At first I take this for a metaphor – perhaps to do with the fate he believes will befall people who frequent drinking dens – but he means it literally. Customers of the bar were being slapped by demons as they quaffed their liquor. 'People stopped coming,' he says. 'They had to close. It seemed like a good place for us to purify with a church.'

He is staying at the hotel because he does not yet have a home here. He plans to build a house, and will then try to persuade his wife to join him. I ask him if she wants to move here, or if she prefers life in Dar es Salaam. 'Let's see,' he replies with a glint in his eye. 'Often it is the man who is adventurous and stakes out new ground, and his wife is persuaded later that it is a good idea.'

After we retire to bed we hear Mabiba's deep voice singing hymns in his room. Later we are awoken by the screams of a woman, piercing the darkness outside. The screams are interspersed with choking bouts of sobbing, and during these pauses we hear the comforting voice of another, older-sounding woman before the screaming and howling resume. Only when the rain begins to fall again is the woman quieted. Ebru and I surmise that such despair could be occasioned only by a death, probably that of a child, but when we suggest this in the morning to a young man named Emanuel who runs the bar in the hotel's garden, he tells us it is more likely the woman was possessed.

Three

On the morning we are to move into our new home, four young German backpackers check into the hotel. Months later we would develop a proprietorial feeling towards our status as the island's lone *wazungu*, but for now we are comforted by the sight of other foreigners. On the steps outside reception we chat briefly to one of them. When we tell her we are going to be living here for two years she appears bewildered. 'Why?' she asks, with a look that expresses both concern for our safety and doubts about our sanity. As they climb onto rented bicycles for a ride along the lakeshore, it dawns on me that this – leaving the hotel, depositing our belongings in a house – is where our move to the island becomes permanent. In a hotel you can cling to the feeling that you will soon be moving on; in a house to which you are enchained by a twelve-month rental contract you have no such escape valve. Watching the Germans cycling away down the dirt road, I can't help but feel marooned.

A taxi arrives. As we are loading it Mabiba appears from the garden. He is holding a tightly woven, perfectly spherical grass ball with a large round hole in one side. It is the nest of a weaver bird. 'You see what God has made His creatures capable of,' he says triumphantly. He urges us to visit his church the following Sunday. Anxious not to disappoint our first friend on the island, we tell him we will be happy to attend.

Masondole has promised he will be at the house to let us in, but when we arrive there is nobody around. We stand by the veranda amid our bags. From the shade of a mango tree off to one side of the house a dozen children sprint over, leaving behind a grey-haired man who appears to have been giving them a school lesson. The man, whose left leg is twisted by polio, rests his hands on a long stick, powerless in the face of such excitement as he watches the children buzzing around our legs. Extricating myself, I walk over to the other side of the house, where on a little patch of cultivated ground outside a single-roomed house an old woman is plucking spinach leaves. She straightens and smiles as I greet her, and welcomes me to the neighbourhood. 'I don't speak much Swahili,' I say when she continues talking. She welcomes me again – 'karibu sana' – and bends to resume her harvesting.

After half an hour Dickson appears and opens the gate. Masondole, he says, has other business. Not long after we haul our bags into the living room, Yuve arrives to take Ebru to the college. The children mob his car, running after it as it moves off. When it disappears down the raised dirt road that passes behind the old woman's house, they go back to their lesson under the mango tree, and I am left in the house alone.

Back in Europe, when we'd heard that we were to be posted to the island, Ebru and I had discussed the threats that might await us. Crime was an obvious concern. Ukerewe is one of the poorest districts of one of the world's poorest countries, and as its most conspicuous inhabitants we feared we would be a prime target for thieves. A more important concern was the threat to our health. Malarial mosquitoes, typhoid, cholera and the rabid dogs we had seen on the internet would be made more dangerous by the absence of functioning health facilities. With a population the size of Cardiff's, Ukerewe had one ambulance and two doctors. Its only hospital was overcrowded and dirty, and like the dispensaries dotted around the villages it suffered from serious shortages of staff, equipment and medicines. Malaria medication was shipped in every three months, but the disease was so rampant that stocks would run out after three weeks. Hospitals in Mwanza were slightly better equipped, but they were four hours away, and if we were ever to fall ill after the departure of the afternoon ferry it would be the next morning before we could get off the island.

But although these risks were real, I was more concerned with how I would cope psychologically in such a remote environment. My previous trip to Africa, a six-month haul around the western side of the continent, had ended badly, with the accumulated effects of heat, hustlers, Christian proselytisers and phantom Colombian drug traffickers triggering a minor but prolonged breakdown. Now I was to live on an island in the middle of nowhere, spending most of my time alone while Ebru was at work, among people wholly unused to foreigners. Remembering the stories I'd read in the history books, I wondered if we would be accepted or hated, welcomed or envied. Solitude, boredom and the unforeseeable reactions of neighbours would provide different tests to those posed by West Africa, and I hoped that when I faced them my mind would put up a more robust defence.

I take my Swahili textbook and one of the broken chairs out to the veranda. The lower branches of the mango tree almost scrape the front of the house. On the brown earth below them lies a pool of water, which has leaked from a plastic tank balanced among the branches (it was from this tank that Gloria's water had supposedly been stolen). Twenty yards to my left along the red road to Nansio pass women with bunches of bananas balanced on their heads, men on bicycles, and the occasional motorbike taxi. A man in a baseball cap ambles in the same direction, a foot-long grey-skinned fish dangling from the fingertip he has hooked into its mouth.

My textbook was published in Britain in 1970. It is bereft of the pictures and variety found in modern textbooks, but replete with lengthy grammar explanations and arduous self-testing exercises. Although the British had left the territory they had named Tanganyika nine years previously, the book is full, too, of the language of empire – in its first few chapters I am taught the Swahili for servant, hunter, thorn tree, 'Britisher' and 'that cook is lazy.' But it is also systematic and rigorous, and while studying it back in Europe my progress with what is a grammatically straightforward language had been pleasingly fast.

It would be speeded further by the children. As I sit studying on the white-tiled veranda, three boys come over and sit on the step below my chair. Two of them, thin and bony, are about ten years of age, the other, fleshier and round-cheeked, around three. Their T-shirts and shorts, of the kind donated to charity in the West and sold for a few shillings in markets around Tanzania, are torn and faded. None of them wears shoes. They ask what I'm doing. Only one of the ten-year-olds, Pascali, can read the words in my book. I point to a calf tethered to a nearby tree and they tell me its name in Swahili. When I do the same for some chickens pecking in the dust, they ask how to say the word in English. Three children quickly become ten and then fifteen, draping themselves over my chair, resting their elbows on my knees, touching and commenting on the white skin of my arms, or simply sitting on the step and smiling, content to be near me. The spectre of loneliness fades.

On the far side of the wide path that crosses in front of our house beyond the mango tree, a woman in cornrow plaits and a yellow wraparound skirt crouches washing metal plates in a bowl. Above her hangs a line of drying clothes, strung from a nail on the wall of her house to a spindly papaya tree. Ali, the three-year-old, tells me that the woman is his mother. His father, he says, is at the lake. It will take us weeks to work out which child belongs to which household. Many of the surrounding buildings seem to be shared between several families or divided into separate rented rooms, and the women would frequently tend one another's children, carrying them on their backs, plaiting the girls' hair, wiping snotty nostrils or upbraiding them when they overstepped the mark.

Dickson wanders over carrying a Bible. He has changed into a clean white shirt, worn untucked, and grey slacks. He is on his way to church, he says – the church of the Evangelistic

Assemblies of God, where he helps in some way to officiate services. In the evening he comes round again and asks me to buy him a mobile phone. In West Africa I had fielded dozens of similar requests without ever reaching a satisfactory conclusion over how to respond to them. This one, involving a substantial sum of money with no obvious need, is easier than many to refuse, particularly as I don't want to be seen to be throwing money around on my first day. When I suggest he asks his boss Masondole for the money instead, he stands in silence for a while before walking away.

As night falls, the thick darkness around the house is punctuated only by the flames of little cooking fires, one from the open patch of ground outside Ali's house opposite, another off to the right near the teacher's makeshift school. None of the neighbouring dwellings has electricity, and our living room, although dimly lit, stands out brazenly. The iron grilles on the windows and veranda offer us a degree of protection from intruders, but they also tell would-be thieves that we have something worth stealing. When the neighbours retire into their houses soon after ten, the chatter and laughter from around the fires give way to a deep quiet. For the first few nights any interruption to this silence alarms us. Every bang on our tin roof, every unexplainable noise outside the bedroom window has us jumping up to check that the house isn't under attack.

Other than a sudden chorus of howling street dogs in the early hours, the first night passes without incident. We are woken just before dawn by the rhythmic swish of sweeping. I look out to see the old woman next-door rearranging the dust on the ground in front of her mud-brick house. Soon after, we hear the clatter of metal crockery as other women emerge from their slumber to prepare tea. Having bought a few provisions in Nansio the previous day, we breakfast on banana sandwiches while Ebru waits for her taxi.

The early morning air is cool and clear. Rain has fallen

overnight and the pool beneath the water tank has expanded. Malaria-bearing mosquitoes lay their eggs in and around standing water, and I worry that the pool might imperil the children who play nearby. The tank is connected to our house by a rubber tube; another connects it with the mains supply in Nansio. We will never be asked to pay for this water – the tube is plugged into a hole or valve bored into the main underground pipe, and the public water company doesn't know it is supplying us. The tank through which the mains water passes is our insurance against water cuts – the regular one-hour supply each evening would soon become more sporadic, in part because of freeloaders like us – but the valve on the inflow tube is faulty, and instead of closing once the tank fills up it overflows until it is turned off manually. While I am awake this is unproblematic, but if it fills up during the night when we are asleep, gallons of water are added to the pool below.

For most people on the island, piped water is nothing more than a mirage. Only a few houses in Nansio are connected to the mains supply, and only close to the town are there standpipes. People living in the villages and hamlets must rely on wells or the lake for their water. To make this water safe to drink it has to be boiled, and to boil it trees must be felled for charcoal. Mabiba had told me that the island had suffered rapid deforestation in recent decades. 'Ukerewe is unrecognisable from when I was a child,' he said. 'At that time the whole island was covered in trees, but now most of it is bare.'

The sun has not yet risen above the rooftops. Women pass along the road to town bearing bundles of firewood on their heads, or sacks bursting with greens. Their posture is erect, their glide smooth. Seldom do they use their hands to balance their loads. Near the lame man's school, teenage boys and girls queue at a standpipe. Under twenty-litre buckets their stride is less confident than the women's, and a few drops spill over as they climb the gentle slope back to the road. Across the way, on the open ground flanked on the left by the back of Ali's house and on the far side by another tin-roofed dwelling, a group of men squat by a cooking fire. Over the little mound of charcoal and twigs, supported by a ring of blackened rocks, sits an aluminium bowl. The men, wearing long-sleeved shirts and windcheaters or scruffy anoraks, hold their hands to the fire for warmth. They talk in low voices as they wait for whatever is in the pot to cook.

Three-year-old Ali hears me unbolting the veranda gate and skips over to say good morning. He points out his father among the crouching men. A little later, after Ebru has left and the group has dispersed, I walk over to introduce myself. Dark-skinned and stocky, with short, stumpy dreadlocks and wearing a lumberjack shirt and jeans, he is sitting with two other men on the raised porch at the front of his house by the road. Chewing on a twig, he smiles as I approach, a sudden, easy smile that seems to combine warmth with amusement, perhaps at the sight of a white man wearing shorts at this cool early hour. His name, he tells me in a deep, Rasta drawl, is Hasani. He is a fisherman. He and the other men have been out on the lake overnight but they haven't caught much. He gestures to the house behind him and tells me that he rents half of it. Another fisherman rents the other half. He is not an Mkerewe, he says, but a Sukuma from the mainland near Mwanza. He has been fishing on the lake for more than twenty years. He left his home village in his early twenties for one of Ukerewe's smaller islands, and moved his young family here a few years back so that his six children, who share the single-room house with him and his wife Lilian, could attend school.

The Sukuma, Tanzania's largest ethnic group, traditionally made a living as farmers, and as herders of long-horned cattle. But in recent decades, overgrazing, population growth and the gradual drying of the climate have forced many to seek alternative sources of sustenance. Hasani is one of a long line of migrants who have responded to changing conditions on the mainland by trying their luck on the archipelago. On the ferry, mystified that anyone would choose to live here, I had wondered what might have motivated Ukerewe's first settlers to strike out for a place that was so remote and so far from anywhere significant. On a clear day the island can be seen from the lakeshore near Mwanza, but leaving solid ground to paddle across thirty miles of water to reach it would have been fraught with risk. Lake Victoria is so vast that it generates its own weather, with sudden storms whipping up six-foot waves that can easily capsize a dugout canoe. Crocodiles and hippos add to the dangers, and even today, when many boats sport outboard motors and weather forecasts warn sailors of impending trouble, four thousand people drown in its waters every year.

It is thought that the islands were first populated sometime in the first millennium after Christ. The earliest inhabitants hailed from one of Africa's oldest ethnic groups – and therefore one of the oldest peoples on earth. The Sandawe were hunter-gatherers, and they might have been searching for game. They would have either paddled across from the south or made use of a narrow ribbon of land in the east that from time to time, before it was washed away for good by the "Freedom Rains" of the 1960s, emerged above the surface of the lake to connect the island to the mainland. Until the early twentieth century there were elephants and buffalo in Ukerewe's forests and hippos and crocodiles on its beaches, but these would have been too dangerous a quarry for a people who did not yet possess iron weapons. Small game, on the other hand, were easy prey. Antelope, bush rats, pigs and monkeys were unaccustomed to human depredations, and would have made an enticing target for a band of hungry foragers.

Hunting is one plausible explanation for the Sandawe's migration. Being hunted is another. It is possible that the Sandawe were forced to flee to the archipelago by more technologically advanced peoples who were competing with them for resources. Other hunter-gatherer tribes in Africa had suffered a similar fate, pushed off the most fruitful land onto more hostile territory. The scattered groups of Sandawe, equipped with nothing fiercer than stone daggers, could not have held their ground for long against marauding armies brandishing metal spears.

No trace remains of the Sandawe's time on the island, and they are thought to have disappeared by the turn of the first millennium. We owe our knowledge of their presence not to archaeological discoveries but to one of Ukerewe's most ancient traditions. *Omwanzuzi*, or oral historians, played a number of vital roles in Kerewe society. They passed their knowledge down through the generations, giving their people an idea of their place in the world and an appreciation of the travails their forebears had endured. They had political responsibilities – the island's chiefs would draw on their learning while negotiating with other clans or deciding whether to welcome outsiders. And they played a part in the provision of justice – in a similar way to the case law approach used in modern court systems, chiefs would refer to historical precedent when called on to deliver legal judgements.

The tradition of the *omwanzuzi* has long since died out – my enquiries to some of the island's older inhabitants drew blank looks – but in the late 1960s an American academic named Gerald Hartwig tracked down and interviewed one of the last of the breed. The fragments of learning he recorded cover more than a thousand years of the lake's history.

Bahitwa was in his eighties by the time Hartwig came into contact with him. The American describes the *omwanzuzi* as a dour, slightly insecure character. He would grow annoyed when Hartwig asked other elders for information, and he 'continually sought reassurance that he knew more history than anyone else.' The old man's self-doubt might have been born of the chequered history of his family. His mother, who was of humble origins, was rumoured to have been pregnant by another man when she married into his father's more privileged clan. His biological father, the gossip went, was a member of the Kara, a people from an island to the north of Ukerewe who in the nineteenth century were of lowly social status.

Although Bahitwa had never attended school and spoke only a little Swahili, his stock of knowledge was vast. A few of his contemporaries warned Hartwig that he 'did not always provide accurate details,' but much of what he narrated is supported both by the accounts of other *omwanzuzi* on the island at the time and by more recent research in the fields of linguistics, ethnography, genetics and archaeology. Oral history is sometimes dismissed as unreliable – easy to forget or embellish, too reliant on the biases of interlocutors, too distant from anyone who has witnessed the events involved, and generally too flaky compared with history written in hard, solid books. But the *omwanzuzi* of Ukerewe were systematic in their acquisition and distillation of knowledge. To verify the data he gathered, Bahitwa laid out conflicting accounts before a group of trusted experts, who would assess and debate them before arriving at a definitive version. In return for their information, he paid his sources in locally made moonshine or in coffee beans for chewing. To refresh his memory he would ask strangers he met on the road the name of their father or grandfather. Then he would regale them, sometimes for hours while they stood there in the heat, with a few hundred years of their clan's history. Such rigour was not universally appreciated. 'Not surprisingly,' Hartwig wrote, 'some people regarded him as a pompous bore.'

In Bahitwa's telling, the Sandawe were joined on Ukerewe by the Tatoga, a tribe of cattle herders from a country far to the north of the lake. Physical evidence of the Tatoga's presence lies in drawings they left on a rock in the middle of the island – simple reddish lines similar to markings found near the lakeshore on the mainland. But these nomads are unlikely to have been numerous enough either to have compelled the Sandawe to flee to the archipelago or to drive them off it. A more probable culprit behind both events, and one likely to have been responsible for ending both the Sandawe and the Tatoga's sojourn here, is the group that came next – a group whose domination of the lake region persists to this day.

Bahitwa describes this next wave of settlers as a Bantu-speaking people from 'Ghana, Dr Nkrumah's country.' They had made their way, he said, through the Central African rainforests to the region around what is now Uganda. Several hundred years later – the *omwanzuzi* is hazy on dates – their descendants moved down the western side of Lake Victoria, before finally crossing over to Ukerewe from its south-eastern shore.

The reference to Ghana, two and a half thousand miles to the west, is likely to refer to West Africa in general rather than to the country led to independence by Kwame Nkrumah. The migration of which Bahitwa speaks lasted for thousands of years, and was one of the most influential in human history. Known today as the Bantu Expansion, an exodus that began in modern-day Nigeria and Cameroon would come to populate most of eastern and southern Africa, and to transform the face of the continent.

It was linguists who first noticed that although they were often separated by thousands of miles, the majority of the ethnic groups south of the Sahara spoke similar languages. The language of the Sandawe, characterised by clicking sounds, was related to those of other ancient peoples such as the San of southern Africa. But to most Africans it was incomprehensible. Nearly everyone who lives in the central, eastern and southern parts of the continent speaks one of five hundred Bantu languages that originate from the Gulf of Guinea in the west. Geneticists have found that speakers of these languages are more closely related to each other than they are to non-Bantu speakers like the Sandawe. People from countries as far apart as Nigeria and Tanzania, Cameroon and South Africa have more in common genetically, and are better able to understand each other's native tongues, than Bantu and non-Bantu who live in the same village.

As Bahitwa's theory suggested, the languages had spread via a massive migration of people that continued for hundreds of generations. The migrants were driven by the search for food, and in particular by the growth of agriculture.

Archaeological discoveries of stone tools and hoe-like instruments indicate that farming first took hold in West Africa around seven thousand years ago. Farming was a safer and more reliable means of procuring food than hunting and gathering, and as diets improved and bodies became better able to fend off disease, the populations of the new agricultural communities grew rapidly.

With the expansion of these settlements, competition for cultivable land intensified, and those who lost out in the resulting struggles were forced to seek less contested pastures. According to Bahitwa, the first Bantu-speaking groups to leave West Africa were inspired by medicine men, whose interpretation of the patterns made by chicken entrails flung on the ground suggested that the country to the east was fertile. Their path had been smoothed by a change in the climate, which had thinned out the great Central African rainforest and made parts of it less impenetrable. Beginning in around 3000 BCE, the pioneers appear first to have headed south-east, along a narrow corridor of savannah. As the lands they settled filled up, later waves turned due east, skirting the rainforest's southern edge. They and their descendants edged onwards, stopping for a few generations until the land became too crowded or the soil exhausted, then moving on. Finally, after three thousand years, Bantu speakers appeared for the first time on the western side of the lake.

Not all of the early groups of migrants took the easier route out of West Africa through the grasslands. A minority – perhaps the most intrepid, or those pushed to the margins by the main migratory waves – chose the more hazardous trail through the thickest part of the rainforest. Dense vegetation rendered this a much slower option, not only because of the physical difficulty of moving through it but because cultivation in such hostile territory required laborious forest clearance efforts. There was danger, moreover, at every turn – venomous snakes, leopards and the jungle's arsenal of infectious disease threats wiped out whole families, perhaps whole clans, and bogged down those who survived. So sluggish was the progress of those who chose this path that their descendants didn't reach East Africa until several hundred years after those who had taken the savannah route.

It may have been these laggards who pressed on to Ukerewe. Bahitwa reported that the first Bantu-speakers arrived on the island almost four thousand years after their forebears had begun their great trek. He also referred to their fearlessness as they pushed through the forest – they were fortified by their belief that potions prescribed by their medicine men would protect them against disease and wild animals. Emerging from the jungle onto the open, sun-drenched plains, this rugged band of latecomers would have been unwelcome outsiders, regarded by those who had arrived before them as competitors for the land they by now considered their own. They might have had no alternative but to keep going, to the southern shore of the lake and thence to untapped, densely wooded Ukerewe. Such an audacious venture would also have been in character.

The Bantu Expansion would ultimately continue to the east coast of Africa before turning south. As it made its inexorable way, it drove tribes that were reluctant to forsake hunter-gathering onto less fertile fields or into the forests. Agriculture's insatiable need for land and water left no room for roaming foragers, and the farmers' superior wealth and organisation, along with their discovery early in the expansion that you could fashion iron into devastating weapons, lent an inevitability to the result of battles over these resources.

Today, all but a handful of Tanzania's ethnic groups are Bantu-speakers, and many of those that have retained their own languages have adopted Bantu ways. In the dry, rocky centre of the country, not far from the capital Dodoma, huddle forty thousand Sandawe, the last remnants of the people that discovered Ukerewe. Until the second half of the twentieth century they had clung to their hunting and gathering ways. Then Tanzania's post-independence leaders, eager for their new country to take its place in the modern world, compelled them to cease their wanderings and settle in villages. Now the Sandawe too are farmers, scratching a living in the parched scrub. Five thousand years after the Bantu-speakers first set out from West Africa, the way of life they propagated has claimed another group of converts.

Four

Among the rows of red plastic chairs, a slightly built young woman in a pink T-shirt stands clutching her Bible. 'I was unemployed for a long time,' she says, gazing ahead at the pastor, 'but I fasted and prayed, and thanks to the support of this house, God heard my cry and gave me a job.'

While the god of the Sandawe is a remote figure with no interest in human affairs, the deities worshipped by Ukerewe's present-day inhabitants are deeply involved in their lives. They determine whether or not the islanders will find work, whom they will marry, whether they or their relatives will be struck down by or cured of disease, and whether they will miraculously come into money. Like a spiritual Las Vegas, the archipelago boasts a smorgasbord of different houses of worship in which you can try your luck. If you don't hit the jackpot in one, you can cross the strip and try another. In Nansio, which has a population of less than ten thousand, there are churches catering to Roman Catholics, Anglicans, Seventh-day Adventists, Jehovah's Witnesses, Lutherans, Pentecostals, Presbyterians, Evangelistic Assemblers of God, and Winners. There are two mosques for Sunni Muslims and another for Shias. Many of these temples are nothing more than patched-together tin or wooden shacks, but there are a few much bigger brick constructions that dwarf the surrounding slums. Each house of worship throngs day and night with believers, who take their seats on the plastic pews in the hope that if they pray hard enough for long enough while living virtuously enough, their fortunes will finally take a turn for the better.

Neema, the young woman in the pink T-shirt, tried out a number of gods before she found one that smiled on her. Her parents were Seventh-day Adventists, but after her father took off to the mainland with another woman, her mother married a

Muslim and converted with her children to Islam. Neema hated wearing the hijab, and as she reached adulthood she began to be attracted by what she regarded as Christianity's more liberal treatment of women. Three years ago, in a ramshackle tin-roofed building on the edge of town, she was baptised into the Evangelical Church of God. Two years after that, when Mabiba set up his branch of Winners' Chapel, she converted for a third time.

The new job for which Neema is so grateful is as our cleaner. We hired her on Mabiba's recommendation; he told us she had been diligent in cleaning his new church. For that work she had received no payment, but now, Mabiba points out, she has reaped her reward. By employing her for two days a week we have lifted her and her baby daughter above the poverty line (her daughter's father, like Neema's, has jumped ship to the mainland). While she works, her high voice filling our house with Christian songs, she leaves the baby with a neighbour, whom she pays a small fee for the service. At home at night she reads the Bible by the light of an oil lamp, and in her prayers thanks God for his largesse.

Standing beside the pastor from Mwanza in the open-sided, straw-roofed church, Mabiba smiles and nods his heavy head as Neema tells her fellow worshippers of her windfall. The service is conducted in Swahili, but since Ebru and I are his guests – the presence of the island's two *wazungu* perhaps polishing the new enterprise's veneer of success – he has decided to translate for us. This makes a lengthy ritual yet longer, but the other congregants don't seem to mind, and Mabiba, a returnee from Dar es Salaam, enjoys showing off his English skills to his rustic disciples.

Neema is an excellent advertisement for the powers of the Winners' Chapel deity, proof that the church's "I'm a Winner" slogan is not just bluster. 'If someone says you will remain poor, negate them,' booms the pastor from Mwanza as Neema retakes her seat. 'Tell them that poverty is not my portion, it is your portion.' He says this last sentence in English, and Mabiba, taken aback, translates it into Swahili for the baffled audience. The pastor wears a cream-coloured suit over a shiny cream shirt. With his moustache, gold watch and Afro haircut, he has the look of a 1970s soul singer. 'You labour as an elephant but you eat as an ant,' he goes on, this time in Swahili. 'God has placed this church here to set you free. If you follow His commands, He will liberate you from poverty, from disease and from witchcraft. It is high time you changed from negative to positive.'

The congregation stands to sing a sweet, lilting hymn. Each of the twenty or so worshippers is as smartly dressed as finances permit. The men wear untucked shirts and slacks above their flip-flops, the women colourful blouses or dresses. Many of the women have a baby sprawled across their back. As they sing, they close their eyes and sway happily. A few clap in time with the verses. Halfway through the hymn their warbling is drowned out by a series of prolonged, high-pitched screams, which a shouting man, his fury amplified by a microphone, sounds as if he is trying to subdue. In a much more crowded church on the other side of the road, a woman is having her demons exorcised. 'She must have been cursed,' Mabiba would tell us later. The Winners sing on as if nothing unusual is happening.

That God is the best defence against witchcraft is a belief I had come across during my time in West Africa, although I'd never heard it mentioned by clerics themselves. Neema had told me that while she was cleaning the building in the days after Mabiba acquired it for his church, she had been unable to rid it of bats. 'There were many, many of them,' she said in her limited but determined English. 'The ceiling was covered with them, and they made the floor very dirty. The only way we could remove them was by praying. After we prayed, they all died.'

The bats, Mabiba had told his flock, were linked in some way to sorcery, their demise confirmation that God was too powerful an adversary for anyone who might think of casting a spell on His followers. We ourselves had had a bat in our house earlier that week, the first of a menagerie of intruders which would come to include lizards, mice, flying beetles, fist-sized cockroaches, frogs, millipedes, small black snakes and innumerable mosquitoes. Neema, alarmed, had told us that the bat must have been a witch or a wizard, or a witch or wizard's emissary. She said we must pray for protection, and for added security left a copy of the Bible in our house until the threat had passed.

Ukerewe is famous for its witches. When we would tell people in Dar es Salaam or Mwanza where we were living, they would warn us to beware of sorcery. There are witches, or *wachawi*, in every village. They make a living, or supplement income earned from more mundane activities, by selling curses. If you want to destroy an enemy or punish a friend, you can pay a witch to smite them with some misfortune. Illness, madness, crop failure, impoverishment, divorce, death – all these are regarded not as part of the natural course of life but as the rotten fruits of witchcraft. Even criminals are wary of witches – the island's police officers are too busy collecting bribes to worry much about law enforcement, but the fear of being exposed by a clairvoyant sorcerer means only the reckless dare transgress.

The *wachawi* boast an array of baroque powers. The explorer Henry Morton Stanley, who came to Ukerewe in 1875 to have canoes made for his circumnavigation of the lake, was told of a chief who kept a full-grown crocodile in his house. The reptile fed from the chief's hands, and 'was as docile and obedient to his master as a dog.' Another chief was reported to own a hippopotamus, which visited him each morning to be milked. Witches can pass through walls, fly in the night, ride their pet hippos in the lake and make themselves invisible. 'A person can die and everybody thinks it's a natural death,' Neema tells me one morning as she bends to wash our floor with a cloth, the mop we had bought standing unused in a corner. 'But sometimes the death is because of witches. They take the person to their village and make them work as a slave, digging and farming. Normal people can't see these slaves – you can only see them if you have special medicine. The village is called Gamosh, but nobody knows where it is.'

The witches hold nocturnal meetings, naked, to celebrate their evil deeds and plan new ones. Before dawn they descend on the lake to cleanse themselves in its waters. Months later I would hear of a Sukuma village on the mainland which was renowned for its high concentration of witches. The village's name was Gambosh.

By proclaiming her good fortune in church, Neema was taking what many islanders would consider a dangerous risk. Envy of others' success is one of the commonest reasons for putting a curse on them. If the people of Ukerewe secure a job or strike lucky with a bumper catch or harvest, they try hard to keep it quiet. The wariest eat their meals indoors so that jealous passers-by will not put a hex on their bounty. Success makes you vulnerable – if I am poor, the rationale goes, others must be poor too. By doing well in life you have broken this tacit agreement.

Envy offers an explanation for why the bat might have been sent to our house. We try not to flaunt our wealth, but merely by living in a building with painted walls, tiled floors, electricity and intermittent running water, our prosperity relative to everyone else in the neighbourhood is obvious. Further evidence that we have been cursed comes when we are woken one night by an owl that has landed on our roof. For several minutes it hoots loudly, until I get up to shoo it away by opening the window below its perch. The next morning, when Ebru's taxi driver Nurdin, a devout Muslim, asks if she has slept well, he is horrified when she tells him about the bird. 'Owls only visit you when they are sent by witches,' he says. By getting up to chase it off, moreover, I have exacerbated the danger we are facing. When we tell Neema of Nurdin's fears she nods knowingly. 'If they come to your house you die,' she says.

In the days following these twin aerial warning signs, I begin to understand how the fear of witchcraft can take hold. I do not believe in witches, but if some mishap had befallen us that week – if either of us had taken ill, had an accident, been robbed or received bad news from a relative – the notion that the curse might have had something to do with it would inevitably have passed through my mind. Doubtless I would have quickly shrugged off the idea, but I come from a country where few believe in witches, and where if I were to ascribe a misfortune to sorcery my sanity would be questioned. Here, by contrast, the people are steeped in witchcraft. Four in five Tanzanians admit to believing in the power of curses or spells, a much higher proportion than in any of the country's neighbours – for an islander worried about being the subject of a curse, it would be more unusual *not* to impute a setback to sorcery.

And in a place like Ukerewe, illness, accidents, financial reverses and the arrival of bad tidings from relatives are common occurrences. Lethal diseases are rife. A mother who hasn't lost at least one child is a rarity. If you fear that you have been cursed, it is likely something will happen that convinces you that your fear is justified. Dazzled by witchcraft's mysterious power, you will then tell others what has happened, and the terror of sorcery – and the reputation of the sorcerer involved – will spread. But it does not stop there. The terror itself renders it more likely that spells will work. Your panic makes you nervous, overcautious, likelier to slip up, more vulnerable to stress. In the worst cases the terror can drive you mad.

In the face of such dread, God is a reassuring ally. God is backed by millennia of history, by a canon of texts written down in books by well-educated clergymen, by lofty cathedrals and sprawling mosques, and by billions of followers in countries where witchcraft is a thing of the past and success is not punished. Set against a motley bunch of sorcerers – the old woman across the street, the drunk in the shack on the hill, the dull-eyed "witch child" who doesn't yet know the extent of his powers – God is a formidable foe.

But those well-educated clergymen do not allow witchcraft to die off entirely. Mabiba has lived in Belgium and Australia. He is a man of science – a trained engineer, a businessman concocting schemes to build hotels on the island. Yet he tells his congregation that the bats in their church have been sent by sorcerers. His big-city pastor from Mwanza, with his cream suit and gold watch, tells them that the church will free them from witchcraft, but adds that as a back-up they should use prayed-over olive oil to protect their homes. Wizards and witches are useful for the churches – they give their flock a reason to attend their services, to pray hard, and to give offerings in return for God's protection. The clerics need only look at the empty pews of Europe, where nobody fears bewitchment, to see what can happen if people grow complacent.

Just as the priests and imams take advantage of the belief in witchcraft, so do the witches co-opt Christianity and Islam. Ukerewe's Muslim witches are thought to be particularly powerful. Walking into town one day with a neighbour, I choose not to respond to a middle-aged woman who is loudly demanding my attention from the far side of the street. My neighbour grips my arm in consternation.

'You shouldn't ignore people like that,' he says.

'Why not?' I protest. 'She was only going to ask for money.'

'They have the devil in their home,' he replies. 'She's Muslim so it's even more dangerous. A few years ago a woman like that stopped a bus that was on its way to the ferry port. She asked for a lift but the driver refused. When he reached the dock the brakes failed. The bus went straight into the lake.'

Five

Most mornings in the early days it rains, a hard, wilful rain that appears to be trying to wash us all into the bus driver's watery grave. It wakes us at dawn, pelting the buckets the neighbours have placed around our house to capture the runoff from the roof. Torrents of water rush past on all sides, carving paths through the mud. A footbridge across the trash-filled stream that passes behind the house is washed away. On the bank of the stream, Dickson's little mud-brick hut collapses under the pressure, and he moves with his wife into our brick outhouse. Some of the women of the neighbourhood exult in the downpour, stripping to their underwear to take advantage of a rare shower that doesn't come out of a murky bucket of lake water. Their children splash in the mud, laughing and coughing.

Then, as suddenly as it starts, it stops. By seven the sky is clear, the air fresh and relatively cool. Kingfishers and weaver birds chirrup among the leaves. Across the way, a calf tied to a tree turns its head to lick its shoulder. Lisa, a three-year-old with plaited hair and an ear-splitting laugh who lives in the other half of Hasani's house, comes out and lolls on a rope swing that hangs from another tree. The fisherman and his crew trudge back from the lake, soaked, and begin to sort their catch on a canvas laid out on the ground. A woman with a washing-up bowl on her head stops to talk to the men, and after a couple of minutes of languid haggling, fills the bowl with fish to take to market in Nansio.

As I unbolt the veranda gate, which we leave open until dusk, Hasani turns and waves. He shouts a Sukuma greeting he has taught me – 'Mwangaluka', good morning. Ali skips over from his house shouting 'Kaka Marka' (Brother Mark, the label the children had decided on when I asked them to stop calling me White Man). He is followed by his younger brother Magesa, who waddles across gnawing on a small doughnut that he holds in both hands like a squirrel's acorn. Magesa is nicknamed Bonge – Fatty – by the other kids – a compliment, not an insult, in these parts. The two of them greet me – 'Shikamoo,' they say – and wait for my reply. I sit on the step with them and ask how they slept. They look up at me, smiling; although they share a bed with at least three siblings or cousins and a room with two adults, they have always slept well.

Ali, Magesa and Lisa are too young for school, but already at this hour lessons have begun under the mango tree. A blackboard propped against its trunk is surrounded by a posse of young children, squatting over the wet ground. Their teacher sits in their midst on a low wooden chair, the stick he leans on when he walks resting by his shoulder. In his sixties, with greying hair and a wizened face, he is known in the neighbourhood simply as Mwalimu, teacher (this was also the sobriquet given to Julius Nyerere, Tanzania's venerated post-independence president). He set up his school a few years ago. Parents who can afford a monthly fee that equates to the price of a kilo of rice send him their pre-school-age children to be taught the basics of reading and writing. Mwalimu has no teaching qualifications, but such is the value placed on education here that he has some forty students, one group in the morning, another in the afternoon. He writes words on the blackboard and reads them out so that his protégés can repeat them by rote. None learns to read well – even after three years in a real school, most Tanzanian children are unable to read a simple Swahili sentence – but their parents know no better and Mwalimu tries his best, often sitting with his pupils long after a lesson is supposed to have finished.

Nurdin comes early to take Ebru to her college. Children run over from the school and besiege his taxi. There are only a couple of dozen cars on the island and they comment excitedly, stroking the bumpers and peering in to watch the pop video playing on the miniature TV screen where the rear-view mirror should be. They wave Ebru off, shouting 'bye' in English – the only English phrase other than 'how are you?' that most children here know – before returning to their stations under the mango tree.

When there is power, Ali, Magesa and sometimes Lisa come in for a cup of milky tea, which I boil in a pan on our electric stove. They stand around me while I try to write, slurping at the plastic beakers whose rims are nearly as big as their faces. They are fascinated by the laptop screen, delighted by the feel of the cool tiles on the soles of their feet. They leaf through our books, lounge on the sofas, wave through the front door at their parents and ask if they can turn taps, press switches or open the fridge door. When Neema tires of them getting in her way and chases them out, they wander off to play under the mango tree.

Our popularity with the children rests not only on the novelty of our skin colour; the opportunity to spend time with adults is also precious. Young babies here are doted on by their parents, but as soon as they are old enough to walk they are largely left to their own devices. Their days are spent playing and exploring their surroundings with their siblings and the other children of the neighbourhood. They climb trees, paddle in the filthy stream, swim in the lake and wander into and out of neighbours' houses. They make toys out of mud and bits of plastic, metal, glass, rubber or wood that they find lying about, and play football with balls constructed from plastic bags, cloth and string. Interactions with adults are restricted to mealtimes, when they sit on the ground to eat from the communal bowl with their mothers, and to the occasional scolding or beating with a stick when they go astray. Much of the time their parents have only a rough idea of where they are, trusting the older children to look after the younger ones and counting on their neighbours to keep an eye out for any serious misdemeanours or calamities.

Once they are old enough to begin school, children are

enlisted to help with household chores and tend to cows and crops. Many families have a small plot of land, a *shamba*. In the past, these would have been in their own backyards, but with population growth the island has become crowded, and nowadays farmers are forced to plant their maize, cassava, sweet potatoes and orange trees several miles from home. One of our neighbours, Mazigo, aged eleven, spends whole days working as a scarecrow on his mother's hillside smallholding, missing school to protect her maize crops under the blazing sun. Still at this age, conversations between children and their parents are infrequent and limited mostly to practical instructions. Teachers, too, are distant authority figures. They cane pupils who turn up late, brook no questions as they recite their turgid lessons at them, and supervise them like slave drivers while they sweep the school grounds or cut the grass with machetes.

That two adults have time for them, therefore, is a rare luxury, and when we come out to sit on the step we are invariably mobbed by kids. We don't need to do much – listen to their news, join in football games, let them play with our phones, field their many questions. Most of them are happy just to be near us, and they beam with pride when children passing through from other districts stop to gape at us in wonder.

In the early days we worry that their parents might resent our popularity. Hasani, Lilian and Lisa's mother Cristina often look over and smile at us as we sit surrounded by their offspring. Now and again I think I detect a slight look of wistfulness in their eyes, as if they would like to be able to join in the fun. They know, however, that this is impossible – looking after five or six young children, in many cases without the support of a spouse, parents barely have time to attend to the daily imperatives of gathering water and firewood, cooking, cleaning, farming, fishing, mending nets and making a little money. If they do relax, it is for a couple of hours in the evenings, when their chores are complete and most of the children are in bed.

But it might not just be a lack of time that accounts for the distance between parents and their progeny. Life expectancy on Ukerewe is forty-eight years, and there is a constant threat of being carried off by disease or, if you are a fisherman, by storms, crocodiles or hippos. Children who become too dependent on their parents will be left stranded and in peril if those parents die young. In parts of West Africa this threat is mitigated by according uncles, of whom children have many, more importance than fathers in a child's upbringing. On Ukerewe, too, orphaned children are usually adopted by adult relatives: two of Hasani and Lilian's brood are in fact a nephew and a niece, absorbed into the household after each lost a parent. But it is siblings who are your closest kin, and if children can learn to fend for themselves and look out for their brothers and sisters, they will be better equipped as a group to cope with disaster.

Detachment may also protect adults themselves. Hasani tells me that two of his six biological children died young. His mother, he adds, lost eight of her sixteen children before they reached adulthood. When I tell him that if I ever have children I will have only one or two, he shakes his head. 'That's not enough,' he says. 'What if one of them dies? You will be so sad.' Child mortality rates, which have declined steeply in most of Africa, remain stubbornly high on Ukerewe, and are the main reason why average life expectancy is so low. If parents become too attached to their sons and daughters, they will suffer more keenly if one of them dies.

After a few days, our fears are allayed when we see Ali staggering towards our house carrying a large tilapia by the mouth. 'It's from my dad,' he announces with a proud grin. After depositing the fish, which is still breathing, in our sink, I go over to pay for it. Hasani refuses my money with a smile. It is a gift, he explains, in return for us spending so much time playing with his children.

Once Neema has dispatched Ali and his sidekicks, I work to

the rhythmic chants of the schoolchildren under the tree. Now and then I am interrupted by hawkers calling me outside to show me their wares. I buy sheaves of various kinds of spinach from an elderly woman who carries them in a plastic tub on her head, and bottles of milk from a young man on a bicycle who brings it in fresh from a nearby village. Some days I allow a knife-sharpener to scratch our knives with the pedal-powered machine attached to the back seat of his bicycle. The old man is nearly always drunk, and crowds of children gather to see if he can complete his work without cutting off a finger. I decline, on the other hand, the many offers of freshly caught fish, which instead we buy once or twice a week from Hasani at a price below what he could get for it in the market. I also decline a number of less humdrum offerings. A large tortoise placed on the ground before our step, found by a group of children at the lake; old coins; a young goat; a dog in a sack – 'There's a boy out here who says you like dogs,' calls Neema: I go out to find a boy I have never seen before toting a fidgety sack on his shoulder; a hen with its legs tied together; a pair of iron cubes – all are paraded in vain outside our veranda by hopeful or desperate vendors.

Emissaries from God are also frequent visitors. Two women collecting money for their church look shocked when I rebuff them. A group of Jehovah's Witnesses pull out a book in English when I tell them I don't speak Swahili. A serious young Seventh-day Adventist in a suit and tie comes to tell me he wants me to help him with his English. After exchanging phone numbers I receive a text message from him that night. 'My fellow just listen while I some slogan state,' it reads. 'Theft make short life. Anger bring damage. Hate, contempt, jealousy bring sin. I wish you a good night.' I wasn't sure what I'd done to provoke such a barrage, but I never saw the young man again.

The children and our incipient friendships with Hasani, Neema and Mabiba relieve to a degree the isolation we feel during our first weeks on the island, but our walks into Nansio to buy provisions remind us of our status as outsiders. The frequent power cuts make refrigerating food pointless, so we make this journey most afternoons. Nansio's main market is less than a mile away. As we pass along the dirt road we are assailed on all sides by shouts and jeers and laughter. 'Eh, Mzungu!' 'Oya, Mzungu!' 'Yego, Mzungu!' The heckling comes not just from children but from adults – young men, drunk elders and groups of chortling women all join in. Some call out as they pass us on foot or on bicycles, others from the yards of their houses or from the little shops, bars and hairdressing salons that line the road. A few shout greetings in Kikerewe, the local language, to test us and amuse their friends if we fail to reply. Others pass comment on our clothes or the contents of our shopping bags. It is harmless, and we never feel threatened, although on the only occasion Ebru tries the walk by herself she has to fend off one man who plants himself in front of her making suggestive hip movements and others who shout 'hey woman' or 'my baby' at her, but it is nevertheless grating. As the only white people on Ukerewe we had expected plenty of attention, and had hoped that being here for an extended period would give the islanders time to get used to us. But when in those first few weeks we would espy the distant mainland from a hill to the north of town, or when we would hear the mournful horn of the afternoon ferry leaving for Mwanza, which left us stranded on the island until at least the next morning, it was difficult to suppress the feeling of being cut off from the world.

Six

In the market it takes the stallholders only a couple of weeks to get over their excitement at seeing us, and it is a relief to be able to peruse their produce in relative calm. The stalls are thinly stocked. On the rickety tables, sheltered by tin roofs held up by spindly tree branches, there are fist-sized piles of tomatoes, green peppers, onions and sweet potatoes. Now and then there are a few aubergines or a pineapple, or a scattering of fish on a concrete slab. On the bare earth of the shady, narrow lanes between the stalls squat sacks of beans and lentils. Not wishing to appear extravagant, and knowing we will be back the next day, we never buy much. Outside, in shops on the town's main street, we can find packets of spaghetti, loaves of cheap, sliced white bread and cans of *Africafe* instant coffee. Our diet isn't varied, consisting mostly of combinations of fish, rice, beans, onions and tomatoes, but it is sumptuous compared with the stodgy cassava or maize meal, accompanied on good days by beans or scraps of fish that were not worth selling, that is our neighbours' daily fare.

The only luxury we permit ourselves is alcohol, which unlike food is in plentiful supply. There are half a dozen bars in the centre of the town and several more on the outskirts, most of them gloomy hovels. Shacks dotted around the neighbourhoods sell bottled beer and sachets of sugarcane rum. In their homes women brew traditional liquor, a powerful, cheap and now-illegal concoction made with fermented millet, maize or cassava. Mabiba tells us that alcohol consumption has increased in recent years. He attributes this to a decline in spirituality. 'People used to go to church,' he says, apparently oblivious to the packed pews in Winners' Chapel's rival houses of worship, 'but now they prefer to spend their time drinking. One of the members of our congregation told me that when his former church failed to solve his problems, he stopped attending mass and turned to traditional rum instead.' Many of the island's underemployed young men take solace in both God and the bottle – after church the streets of Nansio career with drunks, their Sunday-best clothes dishevelled as they stagger between the bars.

Our own reasons for drinking are different – as well as its calming effects, an early evening tipple allows us to mark the milestone of making it through another day or week without mishap. I buy our supplies from a nearby shop run by a portly woman named Mama Neema. The shop sells only beer, sachets of rum, bottled water and fizzy drinks. I head there in the late afternoons as the sun is setting behind the hills, keeping my mouth firmly closed to avoid swallowing the lake flies that at this hour congregate in clouds over the roads. I am accompanied on my trips by three or four of the younger children, who plead with their parents to be allowed to come with me so that they can carry back the bottles of water that I also buy. Herding them as they wander off to pick up useful bits of rubbish or as they demand I swing them over cracks in the dirt road slows down the journey, but it gives me time, too, to greet neighbours who smile and wave from their yards.

Mama Neema is one of the two wives of a fisherman who spends three-quarters of his life on Ukara, a smaller island to the north of Ukerewe. He owns one of hundreds of small wooden canoes that go out onto Lake Victoria each night to fish for *dagaa*, a salty, sardine-like fish whose pungent smell as it dries in the sun suffuses many of the lakeshore settlements. The fishermen lure their prey with floating kerosene lamps, whose treacherous glow neither the fish nor the insects and plankton they feed on can resist. Long, golden lines of these lamps can be seen strung across the surface of the lake at night, stretching for miles across the black water like the lights of a distant motorway. The four- or five-man crews haul in the *dagaa* in swarms and take their catch back to the beaches in the morning. There they sell it to traders – usually women – who lay out the little silvery fish to dry on the sand before gathering them up in sacks and taking them to market.

Dagaa fishing is possible for only three weeks of every month. When the moon is full, the kerosene lamps lose their allure and the fishermen return to their homes on Ukerewe or the mainland and rest. Their visits are eagerly awaited by their families. The men have nothing to spend their money on during their weeks out on the lake. *Dagaa* are found in the deeper waters, and the camps established for catching them are located on remote beaches or on far-flung islets that are too lawless for the rearing of children. It is a hard, austere life, relieved only by the occasional cigarette or joint, or by an afternoon dalliance with a prostitute. When the fishermen return to their families they splash out on gifts. They bring foam mattresses, tin pans, second-hand T-shirts and dresses – whatever they can find in the markets. They bring sacks of dried fish so that their children will have protein for a few days. On other nights their wives go to bed by nine or ten, but in the week of the full moon, their yards bathed in free light from above, they stay up until after midnight, chatting and laughing and listening to the music that plays on the men's crackly radios.

Mama Neema's husband visits her for a few days every full moon, leaving his other wife on Ukara. All three are Christians, but although their church frowns on their marital arrangements it is legal in Tanzania for men to take more than one wife, and it is thought that one in four women is involved in such a marriage. In pre-colonial Ukerewe the ability to take care of multiple wives conferred prestige on a man, and polygyny is still a symbol of wealth and status. Women are allowed only one spouse, but they have a theoretical veto over their husband's choice of additional partners. If an intended second or third wife is 'of notoriously bad character,' or 'likely to introduce grave discord into the household,' the first wife may inform the marriage registrar of her disapproval. Some men circumvent this obstacle – and the opprobrium of their church – by taking mistresses instead of formal second wives, and the custom is frequently a source of conflict. But Mama Neema has no objection to her husband's arrangements – he helps her financially when she needs it, and she and her children have a friendly relationship with their Ukara counterparts.

One evening when I am returning from one of these beer-runs, I am called over to chat by a man sitting in front of the house on the far side of Hasani's. As the children continue on their way, balancing the bottles of water on their heads, he pulls up a stool for me and welcomes me to the neighbourhood. His name is Centurio. He is in his early forties, tall and thin, with bright eyes, a broad smile and close-cropped hair greying at the temples. He speaks fluent English, and when I express my admiration he explains that unlike most people on the island, he received a good education in a Catholic seminary. Like me, he says, he is a stranger here. He is a member of the Zinza ethnic group, from the mainland west of Mwanza. He can understand Kikerewe 'because our languages are similar,' but like us he is reminded regularly that he is an outsider. 'How's the evening, Mzinza?' people call as they pass along the road, or 'Mzinza, how are the times?' Some, more brusquely, just shout, 'Eh, Mzinza.' Their tone is friendly but amused, and Centurio's replies are tinged with impatience, as if he is frustrated that the islanders should consider themselves his superior simply because his people are a minority here.

He tells me a little of his life. After the sudden death of his father when he was seventeen, he was forced to quit the seminary school and fend for himself. For a few years he farmed peanuts near his home town of Sengerema on the mainland, but as a relatively well-educated young man he had ambitions beyond farming. When a fisherman nephew told him there was money to be made on the islands, he decided to try his luck. He set up as a shopkeeper on Kweru Mto, an islet some miles east of Ukerewe. He acquired a patch of land and built a wooden hut. 'Twelve years ago it was just grass,' he says, 'there were very few people there so I got the land for free.' He lived in one half of the hut and had his shop in the other, selling cigarettes, liquor, condoms and other sundries to fishermen and the women who serviced them.

For a while business was good. In a place with no police, however, crime was rampant. As the only Zinza on the island, Centurio was more vulnerable than most, and he couldn't rely on local people to stand up for him. Burglars looted his shop three times in five years. Each time he had to start afresh, draining his meagre savings to replenish his stock. To protect himself he had the idea of going into politics, in the hope that as the island's only authority figure he might be accorded more respect. He ran for office as hamlet chairman of Kweru Mto and its neighbouring islet, Busyengere, a few hundred yards to the south. Twice he failed – 'as a stranger it is difficult to persuade the people here to vote for you,' he says – but on the third attempt he was successful, and in his seven years in power the thieves have left him alone.

His role as chairman involves registering newcomers to the islands and resolving disputes. I ask him if the position is lucrative as well as protective. 'I judge each case according to the rules,' he replies proudly. 'I never take bribes. For five years I haven't even received my salary.' The Lake Victoria region is a stronghold of Tanzania's main opposition group, the Party for Democracy and Development. The party has never come close to wresting nationwide power from the Party of the Revolution and is strapped for cash, but immunity to crime is more valuable to Centurio than the nominal salary he is supposed to receive, and he believes his move into local politics kept him in business.

A tall young woman wearing an olive-green dress and a scarf wrapped around the top of her head comes out of the house behind us. Centurio introduces her as his wife without telling me her name. Pretty, and much younger than him, with light brown skin and large, dark eyes, she is a Kerewe, a native of the islands. A year ago, Centurio tells me, she and their three young children moved from Kweru Mto to Ukerewe itself, so that the two eldest could attend school. He stayed on Kweru alone, and sent them money every month.

Then disaster struck. Centurio fell ill with malaria and typhoid. Both diseases – the former borne by mosquitoes, the latter by contaminated food or water – are common in Ukerewe, and malaria in particular is responsible for large numbers of deaths. By the time they reach adulthood, most islanders have weathered enough bouts of the disease to develop a degree of immunity to its most destructive effects, but when contracted simultaneously with typhoid it can be dangerous. On Kweru Mto there are no health care facilities, and when his condition deteriorated he was brought to Ukerewe by boat. When he arrived he was told that the island's supplies of malaria medication had run out, and he had to board another boat to Mwanza in search of treatment. By this time his life was at risk, and he ended up spending many weeks in hospital, all funded out of his own pocket. Eventually, after losing several stone in weight, he recovered, but to pay for his treatment his wife had had to sell off all his stock at reduced prices. When he returned to Ukerewe he was almost penniless.

He has been back here for a few weeks now, he tells me as dusk rushes in and the clouds of flies thicken above our heads, but he still hasn't been to Kweru Mto. For sustenance the family is relying on food from its *shamba* and cash from the business his wife runs, buying a few handfuls of tomatoes every day in the market and selling them in piles of three outside their house for a small mark-up. To get back on his feet Centurio is planning to sell his hut in Kweru and open a shop in Nansio. He knows Ukerewe's economy is floundering but, perhaps shaken by his brush with death, he wants to be closer to his family.

First, though, he must visit Kweru Mto to let people know his hut is for sale. He invites me to join him on the trip, and when I tell him I'm free whenever suits him, we arrange to go the next morning.

Seven

After rising early, Ebru and I walk with Centurio to Nansio's bus stand. The stand is a patch of open ground to the north of the town dotted with a few battered saloon cars which constitute the island's fleet of shared taxis. These cars ply fixed routes, each of which ends at a little port from which ferries depart to the smaller islands. The bus stand also boasts a single actual bus, a decrepit orange contraption which travels daily to the south-easternmost tip of the island, where it boards a small pontoon ferry and heads in the direction of Bunda and the Serengeti on the mainland.

We climb into a taxi bound for Kitare, the point of departure for boats serving islets to the northeast (our neighbours refer to the rest of the archipelago as "the islands", as if Ukerewe itself were some great continental landmass). The three of us share the ride with four other passengers and the driver. It takes us northwards, leaving the paved road behind to bounce along a wide but rutted dirt track whose gradual rise affords us a sweeping view of the lake to our right. In the distance, blue and hazy in the morning sunlight, Centurio points out a row of three tiny islands, huddled together in the calm, glistening waters. The one in the middle, he says, is Kweru Mto. It is the smallest of the three, a mere swelling on the lake's surface, like the arched back of a dolphin. So low is its highest point that from this distance it appears that it would take only a small rise in the water level to leave most of it submerged.

Reduced rainfall has led to a gradual subsidence in the level of the lake in the past half-century, but there have been signs of a resurgence since a sharp, drought-induced decline in the early 2000s. Such fluctuations are nothing new, for Lake Victoria is an unusually shallow body of water. Although it is the world's second largest lake when measured by surface area, in terms of volume it only just makes the world's top ten. In Africa alone, Lake Malawi, which laps Tanzania's southern border, holds three times as much water. Lake Tanganyika, a few hundred miles west of here, holds almost seven times as much. Lake Victoria spans a greater area than both of these lakes put together, but its deepest point is just eighty metres below the surface, and its average depth half that (parts of Lake Tanganyika are fifteen hundred metres deep). From time to time under the equatorial sun the lake has completely dried up. The last time this happened was fifteen thousand years ago, the result of a prolonged and severe drought that desiccated Africa and much of Asia. Other African lakes, such as the giant but long-extinct Lake Makgadikgadi and the still-shrinking Lake Chad, once the biggest of them all, have never recovered from such catastrophes. But Lake Victoria proved more resilient, and after remaining dehydrated for almost three millennia it slowly refilled.

As the waters crept back in, the number of living organisms also recovered. The tropical environment was favourable to rapid procreation, and the newly flush lake was populated at an extraordinary speed. By the beginning of the twentieth century it had become one of the most species-diverse bodies of freshwater on earth, and scientists came from far and wide to study its denizens.

The creature that was most emblematic of this biodiversity was a small fish so ancient that it likely dates to a time when Africa formed part of a single, southern hemisphere super-continent – the fish is found in India and Latin America as well as Africa, but as a freshwater dweller it cannot cross oceans. In Lake Victoria the fish's ancestry has been traced to just four or five species, which are thought to have filtered in from nearby lakes Edward or Kivu as water levels rose. These pioneers dispersed to the farthest reaches of the slowly filling lake. As they scattered they reproduced, and the fry that survived were those that were best adapted to the new environments. In some areas it was an advantage to be a particular colour to lure mates or hide from predators, or a particular size or shape to hunt down prey. The fish's diets also altered depending on what was on hand locally, and their sheltering strategies adapted to the availability of cover.

Many organisms take aeons to evolve into new species – it took the Galápagos finches that sparked Charles Darwin's theories two million years to mutate from one species into a dozen. But the four or five fish species that entered Lake Victoria as it refilled multiplied to five hundred in just twelve thousand years – a new species, on average, every three decades. The lake was an ecological marvel. The evolutionary biologist Tijs Goldschmidt, who on one occasion grew so bored with discovering new fish that he dropped an unnamed purple and black specimen back into the water whose like would never be caught again, dubbed the lake Darwin's Dreampond.

The animal in question, prized by tropical fish collectors, is the cichlid. Most of Lake Victoria's cichlids are members of the haplochromine genus, known by aficionados as Haps. The name, which derives from Greek and means simple or singular, is misleading. For the cichlids (pronounced sik-lids) are anything but singular, and it is their variety – particularly the variety of their colours – that attracts the hobbyists. Among the hundreds of haplochromines that have inhabited the lake there are species of every hue. There is the Fischeri Hap, collected in the 1880s by a German naturalist, which is silvery blue with a dark grey stripe stretching the length of its body. The Katunzii Hap, named after a Mwanza fisheries officer, is green and white with an orange tail fin, while the boulder-dwelling Igneopinnis Hap is striped orange and black like a tiger. The Sphex Hap is distinguished by its black-and-yellow chessboard pattern, the Red Tridens of the deep waters of the Mwanza Gulf by its scarlet body and yellow tail fin. And there are hundreds more, not all of them named, some sporting all the colours of the rainbow, others changing colour depending on breeding cycles.

But while scientists and collectors cherished the cichlids, local people were traditionally less enthusiastic. The inhabitants of Ukerewe considered them too small and bony for good eating. They preferred the *enkorobondo*, a sardine caught in the island's rivers when they were swollen by heavy rains, the *kamongo*, an eel-like lungfish whose sharp teeth severed many a fisherman's finger, and the lake's various catfish – the long-lived *clarias*, the night-swimming *mbofu*, and the *gogogo*, which could pull out the flesh of a snail without breaking its shell. Of the hundreds of species of *furu*, as the cichlids were known in Swahili, only the blue-tailed tilapia known as *ngege* was regarded as palatable.

Until the end of the nineteenth century, fishing was no more than a sideline for those living in the archipelago. Their main activity was farming, their primary food sources millet and sorghum. Most families lived away from the lake, in the interior of the islands and fished for just a couple of months each year when there was no cultivation to be done. They fished from the beaches, or from little wooden rafts or dugout canoes. They used a variety of techniques – carved wooden hooks and spears, fence traps, sisal nets, and papyrus basket traps like those once used three thousand miles down the Nile in ancient Egypt. They had no need to fish in the perilous deeper waters; in the shallows there was enough for everyone. 'You used to be able to stand on the beach and fish,' Mabiba had told me. 'In my father's time you could catch them with your bare hands.'

It was only when the lands around the lake were colonised – the northern shores by the British, the southern, briefly, by the Germans – that fishing became a full-time occupation. Colonial officials sent from Europe to occupy East Africa were expected to make money for their empires, or at least to balance the books while they clung onto or expanded their territory. On land they did this by extracting minerals, and by encouraging or demanding the cultivation of cash crops for export. On the lake they did it by transforming fishing from a subsistence into a commercial enterprise.

New technologies speeded this shift. For fishermen whose goal was to catch a few *ningu* carp or *kamongo* from time to time to supplement their family's diet, spears and papyrus baskets were the only tools needed. But if the objective was to create a fishery that not only fed local populations but brought in export revenue, more efficient methods would have to be deployed. In 1905 the British imported flax gillnets to East Africa – large nets that hung vertically in the water and entangled anything that swam into them. Cheap, durable and able to trap huge numbers of fish, their use quickly spread around the lake. Further technological advances followed. Sail-propelled dhows brought by Arab traders from the coast enabled fishermen to hunt in deeper waters and to move faster in search of fruitful fishing grounds. New railways that linked the lake's main cities of Mwanza and Kisumu to the Indian Ocean allowed their haul to be sold in the markets of Nairobi, Mombasa and Dar es Salaam.

Catch sizes, particularly of the popular *ngege* tilapia, exploded. Fishermen descended on the lake from other parts of Central and East Africa, attracted by the precious opportunity to earn cash and upgrade their living standards. They were organised into fleets, with boat owners for the first time hiring labour. The region's farmers, meanwhile, laid down their hoes and picked up nets. The population around the lake swelled, both because of migration and because improved diets and public health advances introduced by the Europeans slashed mortality rates.

But the boom could not last. A colonial official had written at the turn of the century that, 'The native methods do not catch *ngege* in any appreciable numbers.' The newer techniques, on the other hand, proved brutally efficient, and quickly took their toll on fish stocks. Ten years after flax gillnets were first draped in the lake, catch rates began to decline. Fishermen who in 1916 had been hauling in a hundred *ngege* in a net on a good night were catching just five per net ten years later. They responded by using nets with smaller mesh sizes, which as well as catching adult fish also hoovered up young fish that hadn't reached reproductive age. Yet the catch rate continued to fall. By 1950 a fishing crew was lucky if during a whole night on the lake it caught a single *ngege*. By 1955 the species was commercially extinct, and catfish and other larger species were also in precipitous decline.

The enormous costs to Britain of fighting the Second World War had made it more important than ever for its colonies to raise revenues. But their business plan for Lake Victoria had gone awry. The lake was no longer bringing in money, and the people living on and around it no longer had enough to eat. Casting around for solutions, the colonisers' gaze alighted on the cichlids. With the exception of the *ngege*, most cichlid species, too small even for the nets with reduced mesh sizes, had survived the fishing boom, and the British sought a way of turning their bony flesh into something of economic value. For this they needed a predator, which would thrive by eating the cichlids and would itself be attractive for regional markets. After much debate between scientists over the wisdom of introducing a voracious new species into a complex tropical ecosystem, a fish was selected which, although never before seen in Lake Victoria, had flourished farther down the Nile. The impact of this choice would come to dwarf that of the flax gillnets – the fish would haul the lake into the global economy, and haul its people into the modern world.

Eight

Kitare was once a bustling settlement whose main street was lined with shops owned by Arab traders. Under a nearby hill, Centurio tells us as the taxi grinds to a halt in the middle of the road, were buried Ukerewe's chiefs. Today the village consists of just a few shacks and a small concrete jetty. The Arabs have gone, one or two to Nansio, most to the mainland. The island's last chief moved to Vienna to become a subway train driver after his office was abolished by Julius Nyerere's government. His palace, a two-storey villa built in the 1920s, nestles in woods a few miles south of here. It lies abandoned, its sepulchral upper rooms reeking of bat guano, a few large drums in a ground-floor living room the only reminder of the days when islanders would drop everything to respond to their leader's summons.

After a breakfast of chapattis and spiced black tea in one of the shacks, we climb down from the jetty onto the ferry. Most of the inter-island ferries are motorised wooden canoes, some twenty feet long and six wide. They can safely hold fifty passengers, but are often overloaded and occasionally sink, providing a meal for passing crocodiles. This one, painted in the green and yellow colours of Dar es Salaam's Young Africans football team, popularly known as Yanga, is only half-full. We sit on a plank in the shade of the flimsy roof, lake water sloshing around our feet as schmaltzy Tanzanian pop music blares from a radio in the stern.

The boat grinds off slowly into the lake. The water is calm, the ride smooth. A cool breeze strokes our faces. After half an hour we pass a low, grassy island, perhaps three miles long. It is sparsely scattered with trees, and a few tin-roofed mud-brick dwellings line the shore. On a long strip of white beach, clumps of women bend washing clothes in the lake. 'This is Kweru,' Centurio says. 'The people here have lived here for a long time.

They are Kerewe and Jita. They don't like outsiders coming to take their fish.'

After stopping at the far end of the island to offload passengers, we putter across the two hundred yards of water that separate it from Kweru Mto. Our boat weaves between slender fishing canoes bobbing unmanned in the shallows and approaches a narrow, sandy beach. Above us on boulders rising from the lake loom marabou storks, one of the world's largest birds. Their black wings are clenched like flashers' coats against their white flanks and their pink throat sacs dangle lewdly, silhouetted against the pale blue sky. Behind the beach, huddled among large rocks, we see dark brown wooden huts under flat tin roofs. Beyond them rises a grassy mound, apparently uninhabited.

The island is tiny, no more than a half-mile long and a quarter wide. Most of the time it is home to just a hundred people, but during peak fishing seasons the population multiplies and more than eight hundred temporary residents crowd into the single-room huts. 'The people here are more mixed than those of Kweru,' Centurio tells us. 'As well as Kerewe, we have Sukuma, Haya, Jita, sometimes even fishermen from Uganda and Burundi and Congo. So they are friendlier to outsiders.'

The majority of Kweru Mto's inhabitants are fishermen. They are supported and serviced by a wide range of other artisans. There are boat builders, boat repairers, net menders and fish traders. There are fish dryers, fish salters, fish smokers and fish fryers. The population is overwhelmingly male, the few women working either as cooks for the teams of fishermen, landladies in the liquor shacks or prostitutes. Like the fishermen, who leave their families behind on the mainland while they are working, the prostitutes come here from far and wide. They move from island to island depending on where the fishing is most prolific. Sex can be had for the price of a can of Coke. It is hard to be certain, since few volunteer to be tested for the disease and supplies of testing kits run out a few months into the year, but it is thought that one in four adults in the archipelago may be infected with HIV.

We jump onto the beach and Centurio leads us through the sandy, boulder-strewn lanes of the settlement to his shop. The nephew who had recommended the island to him had in the mid-1990s been one of the first fishermen to migrate here. Previously there had been seven families living on the grassy hillock. They were farmers, not fishermen, and now only one of them remains. Centurio shows us the hut that was his shop, office and bedroom. A rectangular structure made of vertical wooden planks, it lies empty, having been stripped of its contents to pay his medical bills. When they hear his voice, neighbours emerge from their houses. They are surprised to see him – 'They thought I was dead,' he says with a laugh – and they clasp his hand tightly to express their joy that he has overcome his ailments. He shows us a nearby guesthouse, lest we ever feel like staying here. It is one of the few buildings on the island that has more than one room. Clothes hang on lines in its yard. A large bucket full of lake water stands uncovered outside one of the rooms, a scattering of insects floating on the surface – the island has neither running water nor electricity. The ten rooms, arranged around the yard in an L-shape, are used by passing fishermen or hired out by the hour to sex workers and their clients. Centurio has a brief chat with the landlady, who takes a break from scrubbing floors to greet him. He tells her his place is for sale, and she promises to spread the word.

We continue along a sandy path and climb the small rise. The path takes us past the rectangular block that is Kweru Mto's only church; a rusting car wheel – the church bell – hangs by a string from one of its wooden walls. Emerging onto grassy open land at the island's highest point, Centurio shows us the little plot where Kweru Mto's longest-serving family, the only one to have held out as farmers, cultivates cassava and maize.

A teenage girl in a white vest bends hoeing the hard earth, the morning sun hammering down on her dark shoulders. There is no shade up here – the whole island boasts fewer than a dozen trees. The girl's house lies behind a fence of scrap metal and wood. It has a panoramic view of the lake, of the distant hulk of Ukerewe and, a couple of hundred yards to the south of us, of the sacred island of Busyengere. The latter falls under Centurio's remit as hamlet chairman, and I ask him if we can stretch our itinerary to take in a short visit. He considers for a moment before agreeing. 'There are no ferries going there until the late afternoon,' he says, 'but we can try to find someone to give us a lift. Normally it wouldn't be safe for you. It's a rough place and there are bad people there. But because you are with me it should be alright.'

First he takes us downhill to the far end of the island, where an old friend of his works. On the beach, a crescent of white sand shielded on both sides by piles of grey boulders, are a few fishing canoes and a dozen huts. The huts are the size of dog kennels. Their walls and gabled roofs are made of straw, and supported by frames of tied-together sticks. Assuming they must be some kind of storage container for fishing gear, we ask Centurio who uses them. 'Dagaa fishermen,' he says. 'This is where they sleep.' Shocked, we look again. The huts are no wider or longer than a single bed, their rooftops no higher than my thighs. At that moment, a man crawls out of one. He wears only a pair of jeans, and his bare chest is broad and muscly. He mumbles a drowsy greeting. 'They come here for three weeks of every month,' Centurio says, laughing when he sees the surprise on our faces. 'Most of them have gone home this week because of the full moon, but a few stay behind.'

The woman he has come to see is the fishermen's cook. She keeps a bamboo shack on one side of the beach, with a black plastic sheet for a roof. When she hears us talking she comes out. Middle-aged and plump, she wears a blue and white patterned scarf around her head and a matching wraparound skirt. On seeing Centurio her fleshy cheeks widen into a huge grin. She is amazed to see him alive, and after wiping her palm on her skirt shakes his hand vigorously (women and men here never embrace in public). 'You've lost so much weight,' she tells him, still grinning. 'We all thought you'd died. When you didn't come back for such a long time we lost hope.' She speaks to him warmly, as an equal rather than as his inferior – Centurio, unlike most African politicians, is not the type to flaunt the little power his office affords him. A widow, she lives here alone, surviving by preparing a meal or two a day for the *dagaa* fishermen. Centurio politely refuses her offer of a cup of tea, but tells her he will come back to the island soon to organise selling his shop.

We head back over the hill to the settlement; the walk from one end of the island to the other takes ten minutes. After a lunch of beans and rice in a shack, we make for the main fishing beach. On it there is a line of canoes, among which teams of rowdy young men are untangling nets in preparation for the evening's fishing. One of the brightly painted canoes sports the claret and blue colours of the West Ham United football team, the crossed hammers and castle of the club's crest stencilled carefully by the prow. On another boat is daubed a Swahili saying: 'Even dirty water puts out fire.' The young men stand inside the canoes, picking apart the white nets. They shout at us and laugh. Centurio doesn't translate what they say.

He takes us to meet another friend, a fish agent from Mwanza. In his thirties, with a gold chain around his neck and a gold ring on one finger, the agent works from a hut on the beach. A set of scales hangs from its ceiling. By the door is a typed notice informing fishermen that the factories in Mwanza have reduced the price they will pay for their catch. The agent tells Centurio that business is slow and that the factories have been laying off staff. As well as sourcing his product from independent fishermen, he owns a number of boats and employs teams of men to crew them. Centurio shows us one of the boats floating in the shallows. To its rear, held on struts high above the hull, is a large wooden box. It is full of ice, he says, for transporting the freshly caught fish to the mainland.

Nine

Of the two hundred or so species swimming in the lake, the agent is interested in just one. A strong, fast-swimming freshwater dweller that can grow to the size of a man, the Nile perch was venerated by the ancient Egyptians. The fish was associated with the goddess Neith, who had assumed piscine form while she and the ram-headed god Khnum-Ra came together to create the world. Two thousand miles north of here at Esna in Upper Egypt, there is a cemetery that houses nothing but Nile perch. Consumption of the fish was forbidden under the pharaohs, and when one died it would be embalmed with salted mud, wrapped in linen and placed in an individual grave (a preservation method so effective that specimens exhumed today can be eaten with no ill effects).

It was not until two thousand years after the death of the last pharaoh that the perch appeared for the first time at the great river's source. After a long search, the British colonisers selected it as the species most likely to rescue Lake Victoria's ailing fishing industry. Although it had proven commercially popular in other Central African lakes, their choice was controversial. By eating worthless cichlids, the perch would undoubtedly increase the fishery's economic value. Because of its size, moreover – a mature adult can weigh two hundred kilograms – fishermen wouldn't need to use nets with small holes to catch it, and the pressure on smaller species would be reduced. But introducing alien species carries risks, and ecologists worried that a new, large predator might further imperil the native fish, exacerbating the decline in the lake's biodiversity. Many other environments around the world had been devastated by invasive species, and the effects on a complex ecosystem that had already shown signs of fragility were impossible to foretell.

The scientists lost the argument. The authorities decided that the perch's success elsewhere was sufficient indication that it would cause no problems here, and the promise of immediate economic benefits rendered moot the ecologists' concerns over a hypothetical future threat. In 1954, therefore, as the doommongers looked on helplessly, a colonial fisheries officer in Uganda picked up a bucket full of juvenile Nile perch, strode to the end of a wharf near Kampala, and emptied it into the lake.

For years nothing happened. Fish remained elusive, catch sizes continued to shrink, and the people of Ukerewe grew ever more desperate. In the past they could have turned to farming to feed themselves and their children, but this fallback was no longer available. The Bantu expansion had populated the southern half of Africa with farmers – four in five Tanzanians depend on agriculture for their subsistence. But on the islands of Ukerewe the expansion had reached its limit. Medical advances such as vaccination and the development of antibiotics meant that more children were surviving to adulthood and more adults to old age. The population mushroomed. To make room for and build new villages, ancient forests were cut down. Farmland, handed down through the generations, had to be divided into smaller and smaller plots if each child were to receive a fair share. To produce enough to feed a large family, it had to be exploited more intensively. Packing crops more densely facilitated the spread of pathogens, and ruinous diseases swept through banana plantations and cassava fields. Ukerewe had once been famed for the fertility of its land. Now the soil, overworked and with no trees left to protect it from the elements, was spent.

It would be twenty years before salvation arrived. The Nile perch had been slow to gain a foothold in the lake. It didn't appear in catches until the late 1970s, long after the colonisers had departed. At first the islanders showed little interest in it. Compared with the fish they were used to it tasted bland, and it provided scant reward for the great effort required to ready it for eating. The lake's native species could be preserved by being left to dry in the sun, but if you tried this with the oily perch it would rot. Before it could be cooked, moreover, the perch had to be filleted, and the Kerewe had no experience of filleting such a large fish. They remained indifferent even as it began to appear more and more frequently in nets. Most of the catch was left to decompose on the beaches.

Gradually, however, tastes changed. Government experts toured the islands, demonstrating how the new arrival, which came to be known in Swahili as *sangara*, should be smoked, sliced and cooked. With their cherished native species continuing to dwindle, the people of Ukerewe began to regard the perch as a palatable alternative. As a market for it developed, they also recognised its economic merits. The first catches of the fish in Tanzanian waters were not recorded until 1978, but subsequent growth was rapid. In 1981, Tanzanian fishermen netted one thousand tons of *sangara*. Five years later they landed eighty thousand tons. They sold their haul to businessmen of Indian descent who, with the help of international development agencies like the World Bank, had built processing factories around the lakeshore. The businessmen exported the fish from the airports of Mwanza, Kisumu and Entebbe to Europe, Asia and the Middle East. Once again, fishermen came from all corners of East and Central Africa to join the gold rush. They came from Tanzania, Kenya and Uganda, the three countries that border the lake. They came from Burundi, Rwanda and Congo, and from far-off Malawi, Mozambique and Zambia. By the mid-1990s, fishermen in the Tanzanian half of the lake alone were catching nearly two hundred thousand tons of *sangara* each year – thirty times the total annual tonnage of fish caught in North America's Great Lakes.

The islands of Ukerewe were at the heart of this new boom. Six of the seven original families of Kweru Mto abandoned the land to try their luck on the lake. Farmers from across the archipelago followed them, leaving their crops to wither as they climbed unsteadily into boats. New languages were heard on the islands, from elsewhere in Tanzania and from beyond the country's borders. On the beaches, fishing camps sprang up; some were temporary, others became permanent. Islets that had never before been inhabited now played host to thriving villages. The lake region was for the first time awash with cash, and the threat of hunger evaporated.

It was not only fishermen and their families who benefited. Those with different skills or who were too old or frail to go out on the lake forged a living building boats, making and mending nets, unloading, weighing, drying and transporting fish, and cooking for fishermen. The *sangara* created a quarter of a million new jobs on and around Lake Victoria and generated hundreds of millions of dollars in export earnings. Once again, the perch was revered on the Nile – grateful islanders nicknamed it the "Saviour Fish".

When I'd told Hasani that we were coming to Kweru Mto, a wistful look had softened his normally impassive face. Two decades ago when he was in his early twenties, he had been part of the first wave of fishermen to settle on the island. 'The fishing is better there than on Ukerewe,' he told me. 'Here it's difficult to make ten thousand in a night, but when I fished there I often made a *lakh*' (he uses the Hindi word for one hundred thousand, which has made its way across the Indian Ocean into Swahili).

Hasani had started out on Busyengere, the hump-backed islet we had espied from the top of the hill. He fished from a boat owned by someone he calls his brother (which in these parts can mean anyone from a full-brother to a cousin, uncle or friend), and they had shared the profits. After a few years he met a woman and had his first child, Saidi. They moved to Kweru Mto, a slightly less rugged environment for a young family, and he saved enough money to build a little wooden house in the village. Then he fell sick with a mysterious illness which for six months left him too weak to fish. By the time he recovered – 'I tried witch doctors first,' he says, 'but it was modern medicine that cured me' – his brother had died, and he was left to fend for himself.

Reverses like these can be catastrophic – the Tanzanian state provides no unemployment benefits, jobs are scarce, and banks will not lend poor people money to set up a small business. Many never bounce back, plunging instead into a vicious cycle of debt, poverty and despair. But the *sangara* was a lifeline. Hasani had made enough money from it both to cover the costs of his healthcare and, when he returned to the lake, to buy his own boat. 'It was hard,' he told me, 'and it wasn't as good as before my brother died, but I was able to start again.'

Like Hasani, everyone else on the islands depended on the *sangara*. Fishermen built houses for themselves and their families, providing work for woodcutters, brickmakers, carpenters, builders and painters. Shopkeepers sold them liquor, cigarettes and mobile phone vouchers, market stallholders beans, meat and fruit. They bought tea and chapattis in the food shacks, travelled on motorbike taxis, sent money to relatives and dispatched their children to school. They drank and whored in the bars and guesthouses, and paid priests, imams and witch doctors to make the boom last. Around the lake, directly or indirectly, more than twenty million people came to rely on the fishing industry for their survival. The colonisers' choice of predator seemed judicious.

Centurio's agent friend instructs one of his men to take us to Busyengere. As we make the short crossing, the afternoon sun pounds on our heads, its glare reflected harshly in the calm waters of the lake. Busyengere is a low, narrow strip of land bookended by two small hills. The hill at the northern end is bare, that on the southern end retains a few small trees and bushes. It was to the latter, Centurio tells us, that the chiefs of Ukerewe came to make sacrifices. They would paddle across with their retinues and climb to the top of the hill. There they would slaughter goats or cows to persuade the ancestors to bless the Kerewe with favourable weather, generous harvests and protection against invaders. So sacred was the island that nobody but the chief and his attendants were permitted to set foot on it. Between sacrifices it was left to the gods.

There is nothing sacred about Busyengere today. Our motorised canoe approaches a long beach that stretches between the two hills. There is only a single tree to provide shade, and the white sand bats back the sun's glare, furrowing our brows even though we are wearing sunglasses. The beach is scored by a dozen dark lines of young men, snaking back from the water's edge. They shout and jeer as we approach, but they do not pause in their work. We jump onto the sand and make for the row of tin-roofed wooden huts that fringes the beach. Under a straw shelter a group of boisterous teenagers is playing pool. Women sprawling on the hard earth behind the huts snooze or stare into space. Centurio asks after the island's chairman, whom a few years ago he appointed as his Busyengere proxy. One of the women goes off to find him.

While we wait we watch the straining figures on the beach. Standing in single file, each line of six or seven young men pulls at a long, thick rope that edges fitfully from the shallows. Parallel to them a few yards away, a second line of men pulls in another rope. The ropes are attached to the sides of an unseen net, draped far out in the lake. Squinting despite their broad-brimmed baseball caps, the fishermen wear sweat-soaked vests or football shirts, their faded, loose-fitting jeans rolled up above the ankles. They see-saw back and forth, their lean torsos twisted, bare feet planted in the burning sand. Passing one hand over the other they reach for a length of rope. They haul backwards, then straighten to vertical to gather in a few more inches of the rough cord. Their listing is asynchronous, to keep the rope taut – when one puller heaves back, those to his front and rear lunge forward to reach for more. Their movements are automatic, metronomic, unthinking.

'This is *kokoro* fishing,' Centurio tells us. *Kokoro* – known in English as beach seining – is illegal on Lake Victoria, banned decades ago because of its destructive effects on fish stocks. *Kokoro* nets hang vertically from the surface, in a wide arc a few hundred yards from the shore. As a net is pulled in, its weighted bottom scrapes the lake bed, gobbling up everything in its path. The nets are efficient catchers of Nile perch, but their mesh sizes are small and they don't discriminate between adult and young fish. *Sangara* breed in shallow water, and their young venture out into the depths only when mature. *Kokoro* nets therefore sweep up fish that are yet to reach reproductive age, and during the breeding season they also ensnare their mothers. Fearing that such methods will imperil the perch's survival, the authorities impose severe punishments on those who break the law.

The woman comes back to take us to the chairman. Directed up a small rise, we pick our way through alleys speckled with heaps of fish guts, rotting pungently in the heat. Wisps of smoke rise from makeshift smokeries – the earthy-smelling fish sandwiched between sheets of wire mesh supported on columns of stones, the whole covered by piles of blackened jeans to keep the smoke in. A drunk accosts me and asks for money, breathing rum fumes into my face. Centurio, embarrassed, tries to shoo him away, but he instead decides to follow us, tripping over the rocks as he repeats his mumbled demands.

The chairman, a large, bearded man with a broad face and small eyes, welcomes us to his unfenced yard. Knee-high boulders ringed by glass from smashed beer bottles stud the hard, brown earth. Bleached clothes are draped over the rocks, drying in the sun. Under a little tree in one corner, an old Muslim man in a skullcap sits on the ground repairing a net with a shuttle while a posse of women sitting near him gossip about the white people. Against a taller boulder lean three stoned teenagers, passing around a joint. The drunk watches us, swaying.

The chairman has two huts. He shows us to the one he doesn't live in, where he stores smoked *sangara*. From floor to ceiling it is stacked with wooden racks weighed down by hundreds of bronzed fish. The chairman owns a number of *kokoro* nets, including those we have seen on the beach, and hires teams of young men to haul them in. Each net, he tells us, is pulled in at least ten times a day. The process of laying a net in the lake and hauling it in takes about an hour, meaning the young men are on the beach, rocking back and forth under the blazing sun, almost from dawn to dusk.

I look more closely at the shelves. The biggest fish are little more than a foot long, many less than half that. There are none of the six-foot beasts of legend. The catch is taken via Kweru Mto to market in Mwanza, where it is sold on to traders from Dar es Salaam. If a larger fish is caught, it is not smoked but taken fresh to Mwanza or Ukerewe in the agents' ice boxes – for the restaurants or hotels, or for export overseas. Now and then inspectors from the fisheries department come calling. A bribe of a few thousand shillings – a dollar or two – ensures they look the other way.

The chairman leads us back down to the rows of huts. The drunk man follows, and another drunk joins him. They ignore Centurio's pleas to leave us alone, and again he looks embarrassed, his pride at being welcomed so warmly on Kweru Mto dented by this show of disrespect on its unruly neighbour.

We take refuge in a sundry goods store, where we sit on crates drinking sodas while we wait for the last ferry home. Ahead of us to the west, the sun is descending over Ukerewe. We are uncomfortable at the prospect of having to spend a night here – there are no police on either Busyengere or Kweru Mto, and if anything happened to us we would be on our own. Through an unglazed window we watch out over the glimmering lake for the promised last boat. The chairman disappears, and at length comes back with a young boy aged nine or ten. The boy is an orphan and the chairman has been looking after him. He wonders whether Ebru and I might want to adopt him and take him back with us to Europe.

Below us on the beach, the teams of young men continue their taut-legged see-sawing. The ropes coil up behind them as the little plastic buoys that line the top of the nets jerk towards the shore. When the first squares of net come into view near the surface, two of the pullers let go of the ropes and wade into the shallows between them. They reach into the lake to grab hold of the cord that lines the bottom of the net, which is weighted by small stones. The other pullers begin to haul more quickly, and the men in the middle retreat to the beach. They sit on the sand to gather in the folds of net, making sure nothing escapes. There is no change in the mood, no atmosphere of excitement, merely a hastening in their silent work as the arc of net comes into view. They pull faster, and the end sac, which traps the fish that are not tangled in the mesh, slides along the lake floor towards them. As it nears dry land the seated men jump out of the way, and with a final heave it is on the beach, a sagging pile of shiny white and grey flesh. With neither pause nor ceremony, two of the pullers crouch to sort the catch. They separate any Nile perch from smaller fry of no value, which they will either eat themselves or throw back into the lake. The other men flex their hands, and take off their caps to splash lake water onto their faces and necks.

At last the ferry appears in the distance, chugging slowly towards us from the direction of the Kwerus. When it reaches the beach the chairman hands Ebru and Centurio each a large, pale-grey *sangara* as a gift. We climb in, and watch as hands hard and chapped like the soles of feet dump two-foot-long fresh fish into the prow of the boat. Young men take seats on the roof, their legs dangling at the front. The ferryman's assistant bails water from the hull with the bottom half of a mutilated jerrycan. We move off, stopping briefly at Kweru Mto to take on more passengers. As we head out into the open lake we are escorted at first by five other motorised canoes, each containing a dozen young men. They will spend the night on the water, fishing with long lines or nets for *sangara*. They are laughing and shouting, and I remark to Centurio that their excitement contrasts with the dullness of their counterparts on Busyengere. 'These men will smoke marijuana all night while they wait to pull in the nets,' he replies with a resigned smile. 'That's why they're so happy.'

Ten

On the morning of the 7th of August 1998, an Egyptian known because of his fair hair as "Ahmed the German" parked a truck outside the United States embassy in Dar es Salaam and blew himself up. The explosion killed ten other people and wounded more than eighty. Simultaneously, another suicide bomber at the US embassy in Nairobi in neighbouring Kenya put an end to more than two hundred lives. Twelve of the dead were Americans, the rest Africans. The attacks were claimed by Al-Qaeda, whose leader Osama bin Laden had instructed Muslims to kill Americans in order to drive them out of the "lands of Islam".

Al-Qaeda had been staking out East Africa for a while. Two years before the twin explosions, the *MV Bukoba*, a large passenger and cargo ferry travelling from the western shore of Lake Victoria, capsized in calm waters thirty miles short of Mwanza. The ship was known to be unstable and was carrying twice the number of passengers it had been designed for. Among the eight hundred passengers who drowned – although probably not among the large numbers of third-class passengers who were found to have linked arms as they waited for the upturned ship to sink – was Abu Ubaidah al-Banshiri. Al-Banshiri, an Egyptian, had been a founding member of Al-Qaeda, and was the head of the organisation's operations in Africa. Osama bin Laden didn't believe that his henchman's death was an accident, and he sent two of his men to Tanzania to investigate.

Al-Qaeda took no further action, presumably satisfied that it was just another African ferry disaster. A Ugandan I meet one day on the ferry from Mwanza to Ukerewe has a different explanation. Pastor Isaac, a rotund, grey-haired figure in a red shirt and black leather cap, has heard that there is cheap land to be had on Ukerewe and plans to acquire some of it for his ten children. 'I am trying to pave the way for them,' he says as we lean on the railings watching the ripples on the lake. 'One day white people will find the island, and then it will develop and the value of the land will increase. People need to think about the future. This is why you British and Americans are rich – you put away money and gold for the future. We Africans don't do this. But the future will come. You will be ready for it and we won't.'

Pastor Isaac knows why the *MV Bukoba* sank. 'It was an attack by the devil,' he says. 'It was an amazing event. The ferry turned right over in a few seconds. People could see it from the shore. They said they had never seen anything like it.' When I raise my eyebrows, he presses the point: 'How could such a large ship turn over so quickly? It turned one hundred and eighty degrees, in calm water. It's not possible. It must have been an attack.' I ask him why he thinks the devil might have got involved. 'Maybe some of those on board were great sinners,' he replies, 'and the Lord couldn't help them.' He knows nothing, I realise, of Abu Ubaidah al-Banshiri.

Hasani, nominally a Muslim, has no truck with these supernatural power plays. 'There is only one God,' he tells me as I sit with him and another fisherman one afternoon on a log in the yard behind his house. 'In the past, the people of Africa worshipped this God and there were no problems. Then the white man brought his two Gods here, and now there is all this conflict.'

Among those Africans who worshipped the single deity remembered by Hasani were the Sandawe people, the predecessors of the Bantu who inhabit Ukerewe today. The Sandawe's god was distant and unapproachable, and instead they propitiated the sun and the ancestors in order that their path through life might be smoothed. At night they would dance to ask the moon for fertility in their families and hunting grounds, while to appease the dangerous spirits that dwelt in caves they made sacrifices, shouting prayers as they approached the cave mouth.

Today only one in fifty Tanzanians admits to holding traditional beliefs. Nearly everyone else venerates one of the two gods brought by the white man. Allah came first. Islam had acquired East African converts even before its founder died in the seventh century. The Prophet Mohammed's companion Bilal was thought to be an Ethiopian, who early in life had been taken as a slave to Arabia. Here he became the first muezzin, calling the faithful to prayer in Medina and Mecca. A few years later, when Mohammed was threatened by leaders of the Meccan community after he criticised them for being polytheists and idolaters, he sent a hundred of his earliest followers to the Christian kingdom of Aksum in northern Ethiopia. He trusted that as a fellow monotheist, the king would give them protection. The exiles included one of his daughters, a future wife and a cousin, who on returning to Arabia after Muhammad had fled to Medina, delighted him with their reports of Aksum's architectural wonders. When in later years bands of Muslims marched westward across Africa waging their holy wars, they would show their gratitude to the city that had harboured their forebears by sparing it from invasion.

Islam made its first appearance in Tanzania a few centuries after the Prophet's death, brought here by Arabs sailing down the Swahili coast. But the Arabs were traders, more interested in buying ivory, slaves and gold than in converting the pagans of the interior to their faith. Their religion seeped only slowly into the country, and when Henry Morton Stanley reported back to nineteenth-century European churchgoers that the land was full of heathens, Christians eagerly responded to his recommendation that they travel to East Africa to spread the Gospel.

Many early missionaries died before they could make much

impact. When the most heralded of them all, David Livingstone, succumbed to malaria and dysentery in 1873, he had converted just one African to his creed (the Scot's long quest to find Lake Victoria had also ended in failure). The first missionaries to reach Ukerewe were given even shorter shrift, killed or driven away by islanders who regarded them as rapacious colonisers. As late as 1940, there were no more than two thousand Christians on the entire archipelago.

Today, Christianity is in the ascendancy. In Tanzania as a whole, Christians outnumber Muslims by almost two to one. On Ukerewe there are churches even on some of the smallest islands, and services blast out of them day and night (a preacher near our house regularly wakes us at four in the morning, yelling furiously into a loudhailer as he proclaims his devotion to Jesus). The religion is demanding of its adherents. Winners' Chapel holds a three-hour long service three times a week, and congregants are also expected to fast for seven days each month and study the Bible every evening. Neema reads her copy by torchlight before she goes to bed. When she comes home late after a midweek service she is interrogated by her mother and brother, both of whom are still Muslim. 'Have you been at church or working as a prostitute?' her brother asks. 'Who is going to cook our food if you stay out so late?' demands her mother. Neema is herself a little sceptical about the need to spend so much time in church when she could be helping her mother around the house or on her smallholding. 'Mr Mabiba says that if you don't go to church bad things will happen to you,' she tells me. 'He says someone you know will die or you will lose your job. But I think God is more interested in what is in your heart. If I pray and read the Bible at home, isn't that OK?'

Her new church seeks to control other aspects of her life, too. Mabiba, who regards her mother as an idol-worshipper, has instructed Neema not to wear trousers or short skirts, which

Winners' Chapel considers indecent. Islam's restrictive dress code was one of the reasons she converted to Christianity, and she is unimpressed with the injunction. 'Does it say in the Bible that I can't wear trousers?' she asks me, her wide eyes bulging with frustration. 'God doesn't look at your clothes. He looks at your heart.'

One day she tells Ebru that she is pregnant. The father is a young man named John who teaches in a local school. Neema fell in love with him, but soon came to realise he was a "playboy". The couple are now estranged, and when John heard she was pregnant he turned up at her house to demand she have an abortion. Mabiba had told Neema she must keep the baby, and when she relayed this to John he picked up a chair and threatened to throw it at her. After a few days he had a change of heart and came round to apologise. He told her he would marry her, but Neema, who is no longer interested in him, rebuffed his advances.

To nurture two young children by herself at the same time as tending her *shamba* and working to bring in an income, Neema will need her family's help. Grandmothers, aunts and sisters play a prominent role in childrearing in Ukerewe. When a child's father is absent and provides no financial assistance, their support can be critical to its survival. Neema has plenty of female relatives who could help her, but her conversion to Christianity means she is not guaranteed their backing. An aunt who lives on one of the most distant islands subjects her to prolonged harangues whenever she comes to visit. A few months into our stay her mother threatens to throw her out of the house unless she reverts to Islam. This could spell doom for Neema's children, but she is too committed to her new God to renounce Him. Fortunately her mother relents after a few weeks and allows her to stay. I ask why she changed her mind. 'Because I prayed,' says Neema, looking at me as if I'm stupid.

Despite the efforts of the nocturnal preacher, our

neighbourhood, unusually for Ukerewe, is predominantly Muslim. Lilian, Hasani's wife, converted to Islam when they married. Neither attends the local mosque, but Saidi, Hasani's teenage son from his first marriage, proudly dons a white robe every Friday and heads off for midday prayers. The teacher, too, is a non-practising Muslim, as is his brother, Baraka, who used to be a fisherman but was struck down by a mystery illness and now, his stomach so swollen he can barely walk, spends his days sitting outside his house near Mwalimu's school.

Relations between Muslims and the few Christians in the neighbourhood are so amiable that, were it not for their names and the occasional donning of a headscarf by one of the Muslim women, the difference would be unnoticeable. Hasani has fishing companions of both faiths. At weddings, Muslim and Christian men will share a jerrycan of moonshine. Food is eaten together during religious festivals such as Eid or Christmas, and Christians help officiate at Muslim funerals.

Our only Christian neighbours are the Roman Catholic Centurio and his family; Cristina, a mother of five who rents the other half of Hasani's building and whose husband spends most of his time fishing off distant islands for *dagaa*; and the family of the elderly woman who lives next door to us. The woman is the Muslim Mwalimu's sister, but she converted to Christianity when she married the first of her three husbands. Dickson is one of her sons, and she shares her little house with another son, Joshua.

Gloria had described Joshua as her only friend on the island. He comes over one afternoon while I am sitting on our step with the kids. In his mid-twenties, he is short but of sturdy build. His lower lip protrudes slightly, its shininess softening his otherwise rugged, dry-looking face. Dressed in fashionably low-slung jeans and a slim-fit maroon T-shirt, he approaches slowly, walking with a slight limp. There is a look of hesitation in his bloodshot eyes, and he introduces himself in English as

'Madam Gloria's friend.' I ask him to sit, and Devidi and Lisa, two of Cristina's children, move aside to accommodate him.

He tells me he is a 'colour painter', and that he paints houses for a living. 'I painted this house,' he says, pointing up at our apricot-coloured walls, 'but now I am in conflict with the owner, with Mr Masondole.' His English is imperfect, although much better at this point than my Swahili. 'Mr Masondole stole my girl,' he explains. 'He has money and I don't, so she went with him.' I ask if the couple are still together. He shakes his head. 'He left her. But I can't forgive him – he stole my girl. We don't even greet each other now.'

Painting houses wasn't Joshua's first choice of career. After an unpromising start in life, his future had for a few years appeared rosy. His father walked out on his mother when Joshua was a toddler and disappeared to Kenya. He left seven children, who were saved from destitution when the oldest son dropped out of school and established a liquor store in Nansio. These were the years of the fishing boom, and the store flourished. The brother branched out into other activities, buying and selling timber from the highlands of southern Tanzania and setting up a video hall in a bustling district of Dar es Salaam. Joshua was in primary school by now, and after he graduated with good grades his brother paid for him to attend one of Dar's best private secondary schools. When he passed the exams that were the gateway to upper secondary schooling, his prospects looked strong of continuing to university before embarking on a successful career.

Then his brother died, after a short illness which Joshua attributes to a curse visited on him by a jealous aunt on Ukerewe. Joshua, who was devoted to his brother, could no longer afford to stay at school. He made his way back from Dar es Salaam to Ukerewe, but on a road to the east of the lake the driver of the coach he was travelling in fell asleep at the wheel and the vehicle overturned. Four passengers died, and Joshua was among those seriously injured, with several broken bones and a ruptured spleen. 'I was in intensive care in Arusha for seven days,' he says, as Devidi, Lisa and Ali gaze up at us, watching while we converse in this strange foreign language. 'Everyone thought I would die. I needed a blood transfusion for all the blood I lost. I needed five bottles of blood, but there were only four available, so they used old blood for the fifth bottle. After this I had internal bleeding. I was in hospital for a long time, but I ran out of money and was discharged.'

He went to Mwanza, but felt so ill that he was convinced he wouldn't survive. He too, he believed, had been a victim of witchcraft, the coach crash the work of the same aunt who had cursed his brother. He knew of only one force more powerful than sorcery. 'I decided to go to church, to talk to my God,' he says. God had already performed one miracle by sparing Joshua's life in the accident. Now the young man needed another. He could barely walk, and was hunched in pain as he hobbled towards the door of the church. 'But as soon as I entered,' he says, 'the pain went away and I could stand up straight. I could even stretch up and raise my arms towards God, to thank him for what he had done for me. It was a miracle.'

He continued to pray hard for six months, until the problem with his spleen subsided. He was left with a limp, and doctors told him he must avoid hard physical labour such as fishing or farming. In Ukerewe this left him with few options and when another elder brother, who had assumed control of the family's liquor store, offered him a job behind the counter, he had no choice but to accept.

Joshua found it difficult to adjust to island life. His friends back in Dar es Salaam were doing well in their studies, and the big city, with its bars and clubs, its beautiful women and well-stocked shops, had a good deal more to offer a bright, well-educated young man than did the backwater of Ukerewe. He regards the islanders as unsophisticated villagers, and is surprised that I, a worldly foreigner, have become friendly with an uneducated fisherman like Hasani. Joshua is a ladies' man, and he had impregnated and later split up with one girlfriend in Dar and another while visiting his late brother's timber plantation in the south. For a while after his return to the island he had been popular with its women, because he was a 'handsome boy from Dar es Salaam with good clothes.' But once they realised he was penniless most of them lost interest. 'In Africa there is no real love,' he laments. 'Only one per cent of girls care about love. For the rest it's all about money.'

With even the girls of Ukerewe rejecting him, he turned to alcohol for solace. When his brother found out that he was consuming too much of his shop's product he fired him and told him to come back once he'd kicked the habit. Joshua resents his brother's decision and is no longer on speaking terms with him, but he admits that he still has a drinking problem. 'People here drink because of life,' he says with a sigh. 'If you don't have work there is nothing else to do.'

His new career as a self-employed painter is not going well, he tells me. Few people are building houses these days, and his clients frequently renege on payments. He wants to go back to Dar es Salaam, but not as a pauper – it would be embarrassing if his friends and former girlfriends there saw him in such a state. I wonder aloud if Mabiba and Winners' Chapel might be able to help him as they helped Neema, not only in getting his mind back on an even keel but in introducing him to people who might require his painting services or help him find a more stable job. 'I can't go to church at the moment,' he replies. 'If I go, God will see that I am impure because of alcohol. I need to be free of sin before I go back. I am praying to God to help me give up.'

Eleven

On their way home from school soon after midday, the older children frequently stop for a while on our step to chat to me or make plans for the afternoon's recreation. Among the more regular visitors are three siblings, Pascali, Peter and Jenny, who live in a tiny one-roomed house to the rear of where Mwalimu has his school. The family is among the neighbourhood's poorest. The children's mother moved away soon after we arrived and now lives on another island selling *dagaa*. Their father spends the day fishing on the lake, and when he comes home to them at night is usually drunk.

It falls to twelve-year-old Pascali to look after his younger brother and sister, and he takes his responsibility seriously. Anyone who messes with them is liable to be punched or have a stick or stone thrown in their direction. He once reported his father to the police for spending his meagre earnings on alcohol instead of feeding his children. On good days Pascali cooks two meals for the family over a fire of sticks outside his front door. In the morning he makes *uji*, a millet and cornflour porridge, and in the evening *ugali*, the carbohydrate-rich dough made with corn or cassava that is the island's staple dish. Most days, however, there is enough food only for one meal. The children, like nearly all of their peers in the neighbourhood, sport not an inch of excess fat.

On our step Pascali, a handsome boy with oriental-looking eyes and a high-pitched laugh, shows me his pencil drawings, which he works on by torchlight in the evenings. Brilliantly detailed, most depict famous European footballers he has seen on TV in DVD shacks (these shacks invariably have a line of children standing outside them, peering over each other's shoulders to watch the films or sporting events shown within). Others are of cars or motorbikes, superheroes or monsters. His brother Peter, who is shy in the company of adults but boisterous when playing with the other children, makes beautiful sculptures made of mud and water that he collects from the rubbish-clogged stream that passes behind both our houses. He makes helicopters and planes, wearable mud goggles with cassette tape straps, and motorbikes with glass shards for wing mirrors and riders with removable helmets. Peter can mend anything, from torn fishing nets to broken torches to punctured footballs. On one occasion he volunteers to unblock a plastic pipe leading from our kitchen that has filled with mud during the rains. He digs it up with the aid of a hoe, takes it to the stream to wash it, then carefully puts it back and covers it with soil, leaving the end clear. He comes into the house to wash his hands with soap – they don't always have soap at home – and to thank him we give him a boiled sweet we'd been given by a shopkeeper who didn't have change. The sweet is smaller than a ping pong ball, but instead of putting it in his mouth after unwrapping it, Peter takes it outside, smashes it on our step and shares out the fragments among his brother, sister and friends.

In the early afternoon Ebru comes home, usually after a frustrating day at work. The teacher trainers she is working with are more interested in their side businesses – their farms, liquor stores or sundry goods shops – than in their teaching work, and the fact that it is almost impossible for a public sector worker to be sacked means they can live without the professional development the project aims to provide. The directors of Tanzania's teacher training colleges welcome aid projects because they bring prestige and, often, resources in the form of equipment, cash and upgrades to facilities. Their staff, on the other hand, are interested only when they receive a material benefit. Many ask for grants to help them study overseas, or for generous *per diem* payments. Others will feign interest in a programme if you give them a free lunch or a fizzy drink. Ebru's project is not allowed to give such sweeteners, and she spends much of her time in the early months either trying to persuade the trainers to attend her sessions or waiting in vain for them to show up.

The teacher trainers' lack of commitment is echoed throughout the education system, and it is questionable whether the herculean efforts parents make to send their children to school are worthwhile. Schooling is supposed to be free in Tanzania, but the cost of buying uniforms, stationery and textbooks must be borne by parents. For many on Ukerewe this is difficult – some cannot afford even pencils – but without these appurtenances children are not allowed into lessons. The kids of our neighbourhood are often still hanging around on our step hallway through the morning. When I ask why, they reply that their exercise books are full or that they don't have pencils or schoolbags.

Even when they possess the requisite accoutrements, however, they seldom learn much. It takes ten-year-old Jenny, who has attended school for four years, almost a minute to read the word "mafuta", the Swahili for oil. 'Mmm......A......................fff' – she trudges through the sounds, her usual fairy-like demeanour turned plodding and clumsy. Katondo, one of the ailing fisherman Baraka's sons, cannot add one plus one at the age of eight. Half of Tanzanian children fail to graduate from primary school. Less than one in fifty makes it to upper secondary level. Teachers – many of whom are academic failures who flunked upper secondary school entrance exams – frequently skip lessons. When they do turn up, they teach an average of fifty students per class, sometimes more than a hundred, in classrooms that seldom have enough desks or chairs. Ground down by the futility, a number of Ebru's colleagues give up and leave within a few months of taking up their posts. It is not long before she, too, begins to look for other jobs.

The children's parents, poorly educated themselves, know no better. In their day most children didn't attend school at all.

The expansion in enrolment in recent years is heralded by the government and international donors as a great success story, and the ordinary citizens of Tanzania are swept along by their enthusiasm. Parents on Ukerewe revere education as a kind of deity – so long as they propitiate it with regular offerings, they believe, it will lift their families out of poverty. Enormous sacrifices are made to send children to school. Assets are sold off, loans taken out, meals skipped, illnesses left untreated to buy the regalia the god demands. Parents do not read – many cannot read – the reports of the United Nations Development Programme, which would inform them that 'the educational attainments of children in Tanzania are poor and have been deteriorating in the last decade.' They don't hear about the national surveys which would tell them that over half of the country's schoolchildren report being 'punched, kicked or whipped by a teacher.' And they don't come across the observations of UNESCO, which would tell them that schools are 'neither healthy nor safe environments, especially for girls.'

On Wednesday afternoons, in an attempt to make ourselves useful, Ebru and I teach English to the children of Kabuhinzi. One of Ukerewe's poorest villages, Kabuhinzi, which lies in a shallow valley in the interior of the island, has no running water or electricity, no church, mosque or shop. The only road connecting it to anywhere else is a bumpy track the width of an oxcart. The villagers are subsistence farmers, who eat what they grow and get by on one meal a day. To acquire anything else they use the barter system, the oldest form of exchange: a few hours' help in the fields in return for a bucket of pounded cassava, half a bucket of corn for a cup of salt or a bar of soap. We had been told about the village by a group of Canadian doctors who volunteer to tour the island for a few weeks every year running day-clinics (patients queue overnight for an audience, the lines so long that not everybody can be attended to). The doctors had been told about it by the bishop of Ukerewe, who took pity on the villagers and suggested that they might be able to help out.

The Canadians have proved a godsend, and not only in addressing the villagers' health problems. The few Kabuhinzi children whose parents can scrape together the cash to have them educated must walk for two hours each morning to reach the nearest school. In the evenings, after another two-hour trek, they do their homework by candlelight. The government of Tanzania, a country rich in gold, natural gas and diamonds, claims it has no money to build a school in the village, but it has pledged that if settlements without schools can construct their own facilities, the education department will supply them with teachers. The people of Kabuhinzi live in houses made of mud and can't afford to erect a school themselves. But the Canadians have raised the money for materials from friends and patients back home, and on a nearby hilltop the foundations have been laid for a pair of classrooms.

On our first visit we are taken to inspect the site. The foundations amount to a few lines of bricks reaching just above ankle height, but the villagers look on them with wonder. Having a school in your community means you are no longer a pariah. You are connected, if only tenuously, to the outside world, to its great stores of knowledge and possibility, to the bright lights of its modernity. No longer will neighbouring villages be able to look down on you, scoffing at your ignorance and backwardness. You will even be graced by envoys from the capital – the hapless souls sent here to work as teachers. With them they will bring their cosmopolitan ways, their fashionable clothes, their new technologies and their surprising ideas.

There are practical benefits, too, benefits that will be felt even if the teachers turn out to have only a thin grasp of their subjects or to be uninterested in teaching them. With a school in the village, parents can be sure that their children will attend lessons rather than going astray on the way. They can be confident that they will not be hit by a vehicle, or attacked or raped on the road. Waking up later and walking a shorter distance will leave students less tired, moreover, rendering them better able to concentrate in class, do their homework in the evenings, and fight off the infections that retard the educational progress of so many young Africans.

In the meantime Ebru teaches them a little English. I go along as classroom assistant. To take us there each week we hire one of the island's three rickshaws. The driver is a cheerful Christian convert named Rama. He is a dapper dresser in the Congolese Sapeur style. He turns up at our house in a wide-lapelled black or cream suit and a red, purple or lime-green shirt. Sometimes he wears a bow-tie. The drive takes an hour, along a bone-jarringly corrugated dirt road, and each time we pass another vehicle we must cover our faces to stave off a noseful of dust. Rama spends the journey extolling Jesus' greatness and laughing when we complain about the night-time rants of the pastor near our house. 'He is affirming his love for Christ,' he protests. 'He gets carried away by his passion. He can't help it.' He himself is transported into similar raptures when he preaches in his own church. 'It's not anger,' he smiles. 'It's love.'

At length we turn off the dirt road and onto the narrow track to Kabuhinzi. We wobble down into the valley in our little red three-wheeler, green fields planted with cassava or sweet potato stretching away unevenly on both sides. Our approach is noticed well before we reach the village. In the prevailing silence – ours is always the only vehicle on the road – we are heard before we are seen. A mile ahead we espy a clump of bright colours. As we draw near, the colours crystallise into at least twenty children, who have run from their homes to welcome us. As we disembark they crowd around the rickshaw, a number of them dancing with excitement. They follow us to the brown earth clearing between mud houses that has been designated as our classroom.

The village headman, Innocent, brings out chairs, but

Ebru prefers to teach standing up. By now there are fifty or sixty children, aged from three to about sixteen, sitting on the ground before her or leaning against the mango and orange trees in whose shade the lesson will be delivered. A blackboard is brought out from one of the houses, and as chickens peck around her ankles Ebru gives an hour-long lesson to her entranced, happy audience. As she teaches, using the trees, animals and houses as props, small groups of adults watch from the sidelines. They pretend not to be listening, but are betrayed by the movement of their lips as they silently repeat the English words. Afterwards the elders shake our hands and thank us for taking the time to visit. On a few occasions we are sent on our way with a gift of papaya or a succulent pineapple. Rama often buys a live chicken before we leave – it is much cheaper here than in Nansio, he says as he stuffs it into the space behind our heads in his rickshaw. The children wave for several minutes as we putter off down the narrow path.

Twelve

After a month living in the house, we stop waking up at night with every bang on the roof. We no longer wistfully listen out for the horn of the departing afternoon ferry, or mentally mark off the days like prisoners. We realise that we will never possess our neighbours' indifference to the nocturnal cacophony of dogs, drunks, preachers and wedding music. Nor will we match their adaptability to the heat, the insect swarms and the absence of running water and electricity (some will die without ever having turned a tap or pressed a light switch). But we gradually begin to feel comfortable in our new environment, and to become a part – albeit an exotic part that spends an unusual amount of time indoors and holds strange prejudices against having children and eating *ugali* – of the local community.

We pass the long hours by slowing to the island's pace. Other than watching televised English football in a drinking shack or consorting with prostitutes at the island's only nightclub, the archipelago does not abound in leisure opportunities. The nearest cinema is two hundred miles away, the nearest sports facility or live music venue across the water in Mwanza. You can swim, but the lake contains crocodiles and hippos as well as bilharzia parasites. The filthy old chief's palace is the closest thing to a tourist attraction.

Instead we indulge in less flamboyant pleasures. We sit with the kids, wander over to chat with the neighbours, read books and play cards or chess. When it's not too hot, we break the routine by going for a walk around the neighbourhood or having lunch in the garden of the lakeside hotel. The latter is only feasible for those with no afternoon commitments. The hotel's kitchen is usually bereft of food, and many hours can pass while the chef or a waitress ambles into town to buy the raw materials of your order before bringing them back to be patiently prepared.

A three-and-a-half-hour wait would turn out to be our record, for an order of vegetable samosas. Even a plate of chips would seldom arrive in less than an hour. After a while we take to asking in advance whether our desired ingredients are in stock, but this doesn't always help. One lunchtime at a diner in the centre of Nansio we ask a waitress if they have tilapia. She nods, and we happily place our order. An hour later we see her leaving on a bicycle. 'I hope she's not going to buy our fish,' Ebru says. After a further half-hour the waitress returns with two shiny tilapia dangling from her handlebars.

On the coolest afternoons we hire bicycles from a shack near the market, battered but sturdy Chinese-made workhorses with a single gear and, usually, a functioning brake on at least one of the wheels. We tour the narrow, sandy tracks in the interior of the island, climbing the low hills for sweeping views of the lake and descending helter-skelter through the sparsely scattered hamlets. Villagers stop us to give us mangoes, oranges or papaya the size of rugby balls. Their children greet us with an astonished "shikamoo". The villages are silent bar the rustling of the breeze. None has running water or mains electricity; only a few have generators. Their inhabitants spend their lives farming or fishing, or sitting in the shade of their mud houses, chatting or staring into space.

Spending time with the children of our neighbourhood becomes our favourite way of whiling away the hours. Talking to them on our step, teaching them a little English, and playing football and another game that involves throwing a ball made of plastic bags and string hard at the pig-in-the-middle's leaping legs give me a feeling of usefulness that I have rarely experienced. Ebru and I come to care deeply about them, and for the first time after many years together we begin to entertain the thought – albeit probably too late – of having children of our own.

As our appreciation of the rewards of parenthood grows,

however, we are also given glimpses of its anxieties. One morning six months into our stay on the island, Lisa and Magesa come running over as I unbolt the gate. For once there is no sign of Ali, who is normally the first to spot me. 'Ali's ill,' Magesa says. They ask if they can sit on the tiled floor outside our front door, but without their pluckier companion make no mention of their morning cup of tea. A little later Hasani tells me that Ali has malaria; he had a fever the previous night and has a splitting headache this morning. The pool under the water tank outside our house no longer poses a threat – the mains supply dried up weeks ago and the tank lies empty – but the children spend most of their time outdoors, and although they sleep under bed nets there is ample time in the early evenings for malaria-bearing mosquitoes to bite them.

Hasani has already bought medication for his son. In recent years, impressive progress has been made in the fight against malaria. The distribution of insecticide-treated bed nets and the adoption of new treatments have more than halved the number of malaria deaths worldwide since the turn of the millennium. But the disease still kills half a million people each year, and most of its victims are African children. The drugs, even when they are genuine, are not a magic bullet and they cannot always protect a malnourished little body against such a voracious parasite. Often, moreover, children begin treatment too late, or take their pills with contaminated water that carries other lethal microbes.

Ali finally emerges at midday, and he seems to be back to normal. I check his temperature and it's as it should be – either the pills are doing their job or he has had the disease before and developed resistance to it. But in the late afternoon he disappears again. The symptoms have come back, and he is no better the following day. Early the next morning I see him sitting on the log outside his house, a blank stare dulling his normally lively, shiny eyes. When I go over to him he can't muster the energy to smile or say good morning. The other children are chasing an escaped pig. They are laughing and stumbling and shouting, but the pursuit barely registers on Ali's face. He sits there shivering in the heat, and before long goes back inside to sleep.

The Indian-made pills he is taking contain extracts from the Artemisia plant, a herb used in traditional Chinese medicine. The treatment, which replaced older drugs such as chloroquine to which the malaria parasite had become resistant, has proved highly effective in tackling the most dangerous forms of malaria. It saves the lives of all but about seventy of the tens of thousands of people on Ukerewe who contract the disease each year. Ali's treatment course is to be taken over five days, so his lack of improvement after three is not yet causing Hasani and Lilian great alarm. He spends most of the third day asleep in bed. In the evening he comes out briefly and sits on the ground. He has the same blank look in his big dark eyes and is unresponsive to everyone and everything around him. His personality has been carried off, leaving a shell where once had effervesced a warm, funny, energetic boy. He vomits twice on the ground – a small sign of life – before his eyelids begin to droop again and his mother carries him inside to bed.

On the fourth day our hopes rise. In the morning Ali walks slowly over to our house to say hello. We sit with him on the step, and he says he is feeling better. He manages to eat a small doughnut Hasani has bought him. At one point he smiles, for the first time in nearly a week, but then the malaria sweeps back in and he falls quiet, the shell-shocked look returning to his face. After a few minutes he stands up. Without a word, he shuffles back home to sleep.

In the afternoon he again seems a little better. We are relieved to see him smiling and chatting to his mother, for as well as being potentially fatal, severe malaria can also cause brain damage in survivors. Still, though, he spends most of his time asleep, and still he is wracked in his waking hours by repeated onslaughts of sharp, prolonged head pain. As he watches the other kids tying live dragonflies to a thread and flying them like kites, he looks more bemused than interested. He seems to be finding it hard to understand what's happening to him, and why he can't join in the others' fun.

The following day is the final day of his treatment, and when his condition reverts to how it had been two days previously we decide to intervene. Until then we had remained at a distance, asking his parents how he was but not wanting to intrude, much less make them appear incapable of looking after their son. But with his fever returning and the spaced-out look again clouding his little round face, we ask Lilian if we can use our self-testing kit to confirm that the problem is indeed malaria. Tired out and at a loss as to what to do, she assents and brings him into our living room so that Ebru can draw a drop of blood from his fingertip. As the needle goes in Ali cries – not his usual hysterical yelling when he is scolded by his mother, but a tired, almost resigned wail.

The result comes up negative. Hasani had told me the previous evening that they hadn't had Ali tested for the disease. When someone on the island has his symptoms, malaria is usually the cause, so instead of paying to confirm what he suspected Hasani had spent the money on medicine. Malaria tests are cheap even for people here, but if the results are negative further analyses are required, for typhoid for example, or amoebic dysentery. These tests are more expensive – checking for both diseases would cost more than the daily income of the average Tanzanian, and most inhabitants of Ukerewe are much poorer than average. With money also having to be put aside for treatment, many have no choice but to take a chance on the most likely diagnosis.

The self-testing kits we had been given by Ebru's employer are not infallible, so I suggest that we take Ali to Nansio's hospital for a proper investigation, and to find out what's wrong with him if it isn't malaria. Joshua comes with Hasani and me to translate. The hospital lies a couple of miles away near the council offices outside town. It is a single-storey sprawl painted in blue and white. On one of the walls near the entrance a plaque bears the logo of the Rotary Club. It has been nailed there by a group of middle-aged Rotarians from Britain. These men visit the island for two weeks every year to paint clinics and perform other menial tasks that could just as easily be done by underemployed Tanzanians like Joshua. In the evenings they frequent the town's bars, often in the company of young local women.

For an hour we wait in the heat, Ali alternating between sweats and shivers, before a nurse tells us that the testing laboratory is closed. It's Saturday, she explains, and the person responsible for testing doesn't work at weekends. We will have to come back on Monday.

Ali might be dead by Monday, so I ask Joshua if we can bribe somebody to test him. Joshua, with the confidence bestowed by his Dar es Salaam education, disappears down a corridor. He returns half an hour later, saying he has negotiated a three-dollar bribe with a doctor (a sum equivalent to the average daily income). We follow him to the laboratory, a cramped room with a glass door and a table cluttered with files and papers. Joshua and I wait outside while Hasani holds his screaming son. 'They're going to kill me, Dad,' Ali howls as the needle approaches his chubby arm. He kicks out unavailingly, oblivious to his father's deep, comforting voice.

The results of the tests show that it isn't malaria that is laying waste to Ali, but typhoid. Typhoid is contracted through contaminated water or food. If left untreated, it progresses quickly from fever to delirium, to swelling of the spleen and liver, to potentially fatal perforations of the intestine. It has a higher mortality rate than malaria, and it kills a quarter of a million people every year. Malaria medicine would not halt this deadly progression, but malaria is a much more widespread disease than typhoid and its early symptoms are similar. As I look at the results I cannot help but wonder how many families, too poor or too distant from health centres to have their children tested, make the fateful decision to buy medication for the wrong disease.

Fortunately, like malaria, typhoid is treatable, and the doctor prescribes a ten-day course of medicine. He tells Hasani to make sure Ali drinks plenty of water to dilute the effect of the malaria medication. We collect the prescription at a chemist in town and take Ali home. There are two sets of pills, one to be taken twice a day and the other three times. This confuses the exhausted Lilian, who although she doesn't admit it appears unable to read the dosage instructions on the two brown envelopes (one-third of Tanzanian adults cannot read or write). Looking inside, we discover that the pills are of different colours, and Joshua explains when each one should be administered. Helped by no longer taking the powerful malaria treatment as well as by taking the drugs for typhoid, Ali's recovery is speedy. Within two days he is back on his feet, playing with his friends and slurping his morning tea in our living room.

Thirteen

The episode with Ali burnishes our reputation as the neighbourhood's healthcare experts. Over the ensuing weeks a stream of patients passes by our doorway seeking diagnosis or cures. That it had taken five days for it to occur to us that Ali might have something other than malaria was overlooked, our protestations of ignorance brushed aside. A child everyone had expected to die was back on his feet because of the white man. One afternoon a local witch doctor comes round, begging us to cure his cough.

The bribe extorted from us at the hospital turns out not to be the last of our brushes with the iniquities of the island's health care system. A few weeks later, Pascali's younger sister Jenny falls sick with malaria. This time we know it really is malaria because her father, aware of what happened with Ali, has had her tested at a local clinic. Jenny is taking pills, but her recovery is slow. One evening, after spending the day alone at home while her father was out selling fish, she comes to sit on our step while the other children play. She has a headache and a fever; although I drape a blanket over her shoulders she doesn't stop shivering. When I offer her water she can barely raise her head from her drawn-up knees to drink it.

As it grows dark, she falls asleep. With her father and brothers still at the market, Ebru asks if she would like to come inside to rest on our sofa. She nods, and sleeps deeply for an hour. When she wakes we take her temperature. It is in the forties, dangerously high. Ebru gives her half a paracetamol and presses handkerchiefs soaked in cold water to her brow and neck. We briefly consider taking her to the hospital, but are reluctant to act without her father's agreement and have little faith anyway in the institution's curative powers. When she asks me to take her home, I walk with her in the darkness and leave her by the fire with her brother Peter. We go to bed worrying whether she will survive the night.

In the morning she brings back the blanket, neatly folded, and says she feels better. We take her temperature again and it is down to the mid-thirties, but malaria comes in waves and in the afternoon the fever and her headache return. With what happened to Ali in mind, we decide to ask her father if we can take Jenny to a different clinic to be retested. He agrees, and shows me a sheet of the pills she has been taking as well as the piece of paper he was given displaying the results of her first test. The writing is in English, which neither he nor most other islanders speak. Joshua and I take her to a clinic near our house. Joshua assures me that it is one of the best on the island, although he admits that this is the faintest of praise.

The clinic is old and dark, with paint peeling off the walls, dust coating every surface, and grime on the windows and curtains. There is a strong smell of urine. The resident doctor, a grey-haired man in a stained lab coat, is friendly enough and speaks a little English. He greets me more respectfully than he does Joshua, and looks only at me while he talks. At his suggestion we have Jenny tested for malaria, typhoid, amoebic dysentery and urinary tract infections. The results, like her previous test, show she has malaria. When I tell the doctor the medicine she has been taking isn't working, he asks what medicine it is. I show him the sheet of pills, and he notices that they are for typhoid, not malaria. That the pharmacist has given her the wrong drugs explains her steady deterioration.

Like Ali before her, Jenny recovers quickly once she is taking the appropriate treatment. That evening after we share our dinner with her, she says she doesn't want to go home. We are unsure whether this is because our sofa is more comfortable than a thin mattress on a hard floor in a tiny, crowded room, or because at home she receives less attention than we are giving her, but when we tell her she can stay for another hour looking at books and photos we receive a broad grin in return.

What Tanzanians call "modern medicine" is not the only healthcare option available to the islanders. Many choose instead to use traditional healers or witch doctors. These practitioners are not only cheaper than modern providers; they are also more approachable. In modern health centres, the sick feel they must dress in their smartest clothes to see the doctor. When we took Ali to be tested for malaria, Hasani donned a clean shirt and Lilian made her normally barefoot son put on a pair of oversized second-hand trainers. As patients are told what is wrong with them they sit reverently, the physician making no attempt to grade his or her language to a comprehensible level. Then, after waiting for many hours for an audience, they are ushered on their way, any questions they might have had left unasked as the next hapless supplicant shuffles in.

Traditional medicine is a gentler experience. It is comforting, familiar, part of the culture. Its purveyors are in no hurry. They are happy to shoot the breeze before getting down to business, pleased to be asked to share their wisdom on the gamut of life problems a patient may be grappling with. The experience is slow and calm, with none of the stress imposed by modern institutions. The healers, no more educated than their patients, speak a language the latter can understand.

Traditional healers and witch doctors are assumed by many advocates of modern medicine to practise the same craft, but there are important distinctions between them. Some traditional healers are licensed to practise by the Tanzanian government. Their diagnoses are based on a thorough examination of the patient, and the treatments they use are often effective. Hasani is no blind follower of tradition – he is keen, for example, to learn about the fishing techniques used in Europe. But he is unconvinced that Western science is an advance on older methods. 'Before modern medicine,' he says as I take a seat beside him on the log one afternoon during Jenny's illness, 'people here lived much longer. There were some who lived to a hundred. Nobody lives that long now.' He draws on a joint and exhales slowly. 'In Africa we have strong traditional healers, especially here in Ukerewe. Traditional medicine was more powerful than Western medicine. It could heal broken bones just by rubbing leaves on the injured place. They didn't just bandage it and wait for it to get better like they do today. It happened to me once when I was a child, playing football. I could hear the broken bone crunching back into place. Now we are told we should buy Western medicines, but even if we can afford them, they're usually fake.'

A renowned traditional healer lives on our road. Ntego is in his eighties. He specialises in bone injuries. He learned the trade from his father, a herder so expert he could heal the snapped leg of a cow. One day we visit him with Joshua, who has badly injured a wrist after falling from a ladder while painting a house. We sit on stools in the old man's yard between two upturned wooden canoes that are the fruit of his other trade as a boatbuilder. Joshua, who has already had two sessions with him, gives him a little money and holds out his arm. The healer, thin and bald and wearing a tatty grey vest and baggy trousers, takes a pinch of powder from his pocket and begins to rub it into his patient's swollen, twisted wrist. The powder, Joshua tells us while trying hard not to cry out in pain, is a mixture made up of roots. The healer's gnarly fingers pull and probe. Joshua winces and clenches his teeth, turning his face in the hope that we won't see his agony. After a few minutes the treatment ends, and Ntego tells Joshua to come back the following day for more.

But while traditional healers limit themselves to dealing with health problems, witch doctors, known in Swahili as *waganga*, can cure anything. Whatever disease or injury you are suffering from, a witch doctor will have a remedy. Whether you are wracked by jealousy, bedevilled by nightmares or shamed by infertility or impotence, a witch doctor can rustle up the appropriate potion. For where traditional healers have only the tools of observation and examination to help them identify the cause of a problem, a witch doctor has access to occult powers. 'Traditional healers treat you without knowing where an illness has come from,' Joshua explains. 'Witch doctors tell you the source of the illness.' That source is invariably human, somebody who wants to bring you down. It might have been a mosquito bite that gave you malaria or a broken ladder that led to your fall, but the ultimate cause of your affliction is a curse visited on you by an enemy and delivered via a witch. Without this curse, your life would have continued unmolested. The mosquito would have flown past without biting you, and the ladder would have given way while someone else, not you, was climbing it.

Although they devote their lives to combating these curses, witch doctors are controversial figures. They are widely feared, often hated. 'They create conflict in communities,' says a Christian named Bebe who works for a few weeks a year as a translator for the Canadian doctors. 'They tell you somebody has cursed you, and even if you weren't enemies with this person before, you will be after that.' Only by pinpointing who has cursed you and the reason for their ire can a witch doctor find the correct remedy. If envy over money is what triggered the hex, a different medicine will be prescribed than if it was a matter of the heart. If it was a family member who cursed you, you will need a different remedy than if it was a neighbour. Some witches are more powerful than others, meaning stronger defences will be required. During one of our absences from Ukerewe our neighbourhood's most powerful witch dies. Graves on the island are usually dug to a depth of five or six feet, but for this man, one of the gravediggers tells me, they made so deep a hole that a ladder was needed to lower in the body. Many of the treatments used by witch doctors are similar to those deployed by traditional healers, but others are more abstract, involving singing and dancing, baths in enchanted water, incantations to summon out the evil spirits that have invaded your body, or readings from the Quran or Bible.

Christians and Muslims have a complex relationship with witchcraft. In the early months of Neema's employment with us, her mother, a Muslim, had visited an *mganga* after contracting malaria. The treatment involved the medicine man making cuts in her mother's skin with a pair of nail scissors and rubbing into the wound a potion made with ground-up leaves. Neema, who has faith only in Jesus, had been confident that it wouldn't work, and was taken aback when her mother recovered.

Some weeks later, Neema, by now several months pregnant, surprises me by reporting that she, too, has visited a witch doctor. 'I had stomach pains because of the baby,' she explains. 'Someone in my village wanted to kill me or the baby because of jealousy. They say that if I'm pregnant I must have a boyfriend. I have a job too, so they want to kill me. First I went to Mr Mabiba, and he prayed for me in church. But it didn't work, so I went to the witch doctor. He also works through God. He told me if I go back to John I will die. He gave me a liquid and told me to drink it and wash with it. Now I'm better.' She asks me not to mention this to Mabiba. 'He would be very angry. He wouldn't let me into church after taking that medicine. He talks to spirits and would know I have been taking it. I can't go back to church until I finish the dose.'

I am given a glimpse of the occultists' methods for identifying the source of curses when Joshua introduces me to the witch doctor he uses. He and his family adopt a pragmatic approach to health care, turning to modern medicine, traditional healers or witch doctors depending on the type of illness and on how much money they have at the time. For several days Joshua has had what sounds like flu. The witch doctor, a youngish man in scruffy brown clothes whose breath smells of alcohol, has told him that his uncle's wife has cursed him. The woman is apparently jealous that he has a painting job, and of his presumably lucrative friendship with a white couple. Joshua had already suspected the aunt of being a witch – her husband gives all his income to her side of the family rather than helping his own blood relatives – and he is not surprised by the diagnosis. Sitting on the cement floor of his bedroom while the *mganga* tips a pinkish powder into a cone of paper, Joshua suggests I question the man about his work.

To test his clairvoyant powers, I ask if he can tell me anything about my life. Calmly he pulls a string of white beads from his satchel and drops it on the floor between us. He stares at it for a few seconds. It is late afternoon, and the room is lit only by dusty shards of sunlight that pierce holes in the closed window shutter. Joshua watches on with a smile as the man begins to speak. First he asks me if my mother and father are still together, an old trick to give himself a springboard. I go along with it and tell him they are not. He then tells me correctly that my parents had two children together and that they now have other partners. Couples splitting up is common here, but few adults my age have both their parents still alive and very few married couples have only two children. Next he informs me that my stepmother was jealous, and refused to allow my father to see my sister and me 'because she was worried he would give you his property and come back to live with you.' This too is true. Joshua shakes his head in amazement, and looks at me to check that I am sufficiently flabbergasted. The doctor ends by reminding me that my mother is due to visit us here soon: a few weeks previously she had bought her plane ticket.

Joshua swears he has told the man nothing about me. That the witch doctor had to ask if my parents were separated supports this contention. His more detailed pronouncements might have been random lucky guesses, or he might have been privy to local gossip (although I had told nobody about my stepmother). Joshua, though, is convinced the man is a seer. 'You see?' he says as I rise to leave. His smile has broadened into a grin.

Fourteen

To investigate further the powers of Ukerewe's witch doctors, we hire bicycles one afternoon and cycle along the lakeshore to a small village. Accompanying us is a man named Yohana, a self-styled tour guide for the trickle of foreigners who stray onto the island. Yohana is in his early thirties and of strong build, but his face looks older – his eyes are pale and weary, his close-cropped hair prematurely thin. A melancholy air pervades his gestures, and his breath is tainted with the smell of moonshine.

As we cycle along the bumpy dirt track that skirts the lake, he tells us that he himself has suffered as a result of witchcraft. A few years ago his father died. At first it was thought to have been a natural death, but then the dead man began to appear in his village. He would roam around asking his erstwhile neighbours for food and water, and begging them to help him come back to life. 'It was a magical death, not a real one,' Yohana explains. 'He was killed by witches after he defeated them in the election to be village chairman. "These are the people who took me," he told us.'

Yohana says that the divide between witches and witch doctors has blurred in recent times. 'Witches are killers, but witch doctors are supposed to be healers. They can cure illnesses caused by witchcraft that traditional healers can't do anything about. But these days, witch doctors also kill people, if you give them enough money or cows. They have been corrupted.'

The village is shaded by a thick copse of mango and palm trees. In a clearing lies the witch doctor's compound. The clinic is a tiny round building made of mud under a thatched roof. From its eaves two dead birds hang drying, head-down. One, an orange and blue kingfisher, looks fresh. The other is too decomposed to identify, just a few dark feathers still attached to its desiccated body, its little skull bare. Enclosing the yard in front of the hut are three larger buildings with tin roofs. Before them on the ground sit the doctor's patients, waiting for their medicine to do its work.

As we lean our bicycles against one of the buildings, a patient goes off to find the witch doctor. At length a small, bright-eyed woman in a green headscarf appears. She is in her late forties or early fifties, her high forehead traced with shallow lines. She wears an old maroon dress patterned with white flowers. A mobile phone dangles in an orange pouch from her neck.

The woman smiles warmly and introduces herself as Dina Charles. She has been out at her *shamba*, she says, preparing the soil for planting. She beckons us into her clinic. Above the doorway, which is covered by a black curtain, is a notice written in white chalk which tells customers to remove their shoes before entering. Beside this is scrawled Dina's mobile phone number. We sit cross-legged on the earthen floor, our backs against the cool mud wall. Dina shows us a school exercise book in which she has written in pencil her patients' records along with a tally of how much they owe. Some patients stay for weeks, she says, sleeping on mats on the floor while they continue their course of treatment. The most satisfied give her gifts as well as money. The three tin-roofed buildings around the yard were donated by grateful patients; others have rewarded her with goats or cows.

I ask about the birds hanging outside. She mimes breaking a bird's neck, and says they were killed for use in medicines. Her potions comprise roots, barks, plants and bones. The recipes come to her in her sleep. Her dreams tell her to open the Bible, and the page she alights on tells her where she will find the elixir. 'Sometimes I have to go as far as Tanga or Morogoro,' she says, referring to towns hundreds of miles to the east. 'I look for the medicines in the bush.'

Her Bible lies next to her on the floor, beside a black flywhisk. She acquired these tools of her trade via magical means. Her father had been a witch doctor before her, and until he retired three years ago Dina had lived a normal life, working as a farmer and bringing up her daughter. Her metamorphosis, she tells us, was involuntary. One morning soon after her father's retirement she was compelled by a strange force to run out of her house and climb to the top of a nearby hill. 'I went crazy,' she says. 'I stayed up there alone for two weeks. Nobody knew where I was. Then I ran down into the lake and stood in the water for a day.' She emerged bearing the flywhisk, then ran up another hill on whose summit she found a cross and a Bible. 'When I came back down I didn't come into the village, but sat under a lemon tree nearby. I stayed there for a few days, even though it was raining every day. A Sukuma man came by. He took pity on me and built me this hut. After that I became a witch doctor.'

She begins her work as an *mganga* after dusk. 'First I listen to the patient to find out what's wrong,' she tells us, her voice slow and gravelly. 'Then I start the work of removing the evil spirits – the *jinns* – that entered them when they were cursed.'

The extraction process incorporates both Christian and pagan symbols. She starts by cutting the throat of a white chicken brought by the patient. She lets the blood drip into a metal pan filled with water, then adds a powdered medicine. Beginning on the eastern side of the pan – 'the side where the sun rises' – she scatters the powder over the liquid in the shape of a cross. The mixture is heated over coals, and when it begins to steam she drapes a cloth over the patient's head and instructs them to bend over the pan and breathe in the vapour. In the meantime, two elderly women and Dina's twenty-year-old daughter join her to dance around the fire in the darkness. As they cavort they sing incantations and shake rattles made from dried calabash gourds.

Dina explains the importance of this part of the ritual. 'When I boil the mixture, demons come out of the patient's body and into my own. I can see them – they have no heads or legs –

but I'm not afraid of them because I have met all troubles and overcome them. I send them away, and watch them as they go.'

For her final act, she leads the patient to a nearby crossroads (such sites have been a popular venue for witchcraft activities since pre-Christian times – the Greek goddess of witchcraft, Hecate, was also the goddess of crossroads). The patient is by now dressed in a fresh white robe, signifying purity and cleanliness. Dina summons the 'good spirits' and while she prays for the help of God and the ancestors, the patient washes in a new medicine, clearing the path for benevolent forces to enter the body.

She turns to the last page of the exercise book to show us her price list. It contains a range of ailments – fever, bilharzia, malaria, skin diseases, swellings, madness, fertility problems and so on. She points to a man sitting outside who not long ago was running around naked but is now on his way to being cured. If you are struggling to find work, she can help. Similarly if you are suffering from alcoholism. Remembering Yohana's comment on the corruption of her craft, I ask if she ever uses her knowledge to do harm. She replies: 'Only if people have themselves been harmed. If they want revenge I help them.'

As well as her medical endeavours, Dina also provides divination services. The cost of a forecast is equal to the average Tanzanian's daily income, but since we have agreed to pay her three times that for an audience she is happy to throw in a demonstration. She takes us outside and directs us to low stools in the shade of one of the buildings. She chooses Ebru to be her guinea pig. After covering her head with a black cloth, she and her assistants sing and dance around her, summoning the spirits of the ancestors. After a few minutes they stop, and Dina takes a seat facing us.

'You sometimes have shivers for no reason,' she begins, looking Ebru in the eye. 'Even when the weather is not cold.' This is true. In Turkey, Ebru's homeland, they say that such tremors mean the devil has prodded you, but Dina has a different explanation. 'Your ancestors are displeased,' she says. 'You have travelled too far from home and they are telling you that you shouldn't leave your culture and traditions behind.' Ebru, who worries about her long period of exile, is impressed and slightly spooked, but her admiration is diluted when Dina tells her incorrectly that she has no older living female relatives. Chastened by this reverse, the *mganga* turns to Yohana and me. We have neither had our heads covered nor been danced around, but she nevertheless correctly informs us that we each had a grandfather we never met. Yohana's eyes widen in surprise. Dina's assistants laugh and nod their heads, reassured that their boss's wizardry remains intact.

Fifteen

Witchcraft is often assumed to be a remnant of Africa's ancient past, but on Ukerewe it is a relatively modern phenomenon. Until the early 1800s, the possession of occult powers was limited to chiefs. They alone could manipulate the natural environment by summoning droughts or floods, conjuring up epidemics or laying on bountiful harvests. Chiefs whose rainmaking abilities showed signs of waning would be deposed as their desperate subjects sought a new leader to relieve their hunger. The commoners themselves had no such gifts, and the idea that they could draw on magic to visit harm on others was unheard of.

Like religion, however, witchcraft thrives during periods of stress. The 1800s saw an opening up of the archipelago to outside influences, and in particular to long-distance trade. The old, settled patterns of life were disrupted, and the disruption paved the way for the democratisation of sorcery. Within just a few decades, control over magic had slipped from the chiefs' grasp. Now anybody could use it, and few were immune to its effects.

Before the nineteenth century, Ukerewe had had only sporadic contact with the world beyond the lake. With rainfall consistent and plentiful, the archipelago was fertile enough to feed its inhabitants and there was seldom any need to make the crossing to the mainland. Interaction with outsiders occurred only when mainlanders needed the islanders' help. Driven onto the lake by food shortages, those who made it across safely would exchange livestock and metal tools for the islands' grain surpluses. In the worst droughts the value of Ukerewe's grain increased to such an extent that it could be traded for slaves. It was not unheard of for starving mainlanders to sell themselves into slavery, bartering their freedom for sustenance. These captives would be taken into the households of chiefs, where they would spend the rest of their days performing domestic chores and working the fecund fields.

But once Arab traders and European explorers began to penetrate the East African interior, the islanders' self-sufficiency crumbled. These interlopers brought with them a cornucopia of new trade goods. They brought exotic luxuries such as beads, cloth and copper wire, and technological wonders in the shape of guns and gunpowder. In return they sought ivory, and the Kerewe formed elephant hunting associations to respond to the demand. Slaves, too, became a currency, not only as a trading commodity in times of famine but as a means for islanders to advance their social status. First they made trips to purchase slaves on the mainland. Soon they were conducting slave raids. In the past, your standing in society had been a question of ancestry and the relative power of your clan; now, wealth emerged as a differentiator. Social status was no longer an accident of birth, but could be acquired by accumulating riches. There had always been competition *between* clans and tribes, but now, as individualism began to edge aside communalism, it destabilised relationships *within* clans, too.

Long-distance traders also brought new diseases to the islands. One of Gerald Hartwig's historian informants reported that the advent of cholera and smallpox to the archipelago soon after it opened up to trade led to dramatic increases in mortality rates. A mysterious ogre also started to wreak havoc at this time. Known as Butamile, it was thought to be either a man-eating lion or a man dressed as a lion. Travelling in West Africa in the 1930s, Graham Greene was told of murders committed by men dressed as gorillas, and in Sierra Leone in 2010 I had heard rumours of leopard men who left scratch marks as a calling card on the corpses of their victims. Butamile might also have been a shape-shifter, a being controlled by the chief of Ukerewe that metamorphosed from human into leonine form to pick off the leader's enemies. For several years it sowed terror, heightening the feeling of disorientation in an environment that until then had been notable for its constancy.

In searching for an explanation for the surge in mortality, beleaguered islanders concluded that sorcery was to blame. The recent arrivals had brought with them dangerous new concoctions. Jita people from the east of the lake introduced poisons that could be administered with food – a more covert means of killing than the poisoned arrows used by the Kerewe. Sukuma elephant hunters brought protective potions whose effectiveness outstripped that of anything deployed by chiefs. A group of Zinza clans – Centurio's ancestors – made the journey across the lake and used their powers of sorcery to kill their new neighbours and take over their property. Faced with this influx of magical weaponry, the chiefs were no longer able to protect their subjects. Instead of acting to tackle the threat, the island's most powerful ruler took to consulting the Zinza medicine men when resolving disputes. By the time one of his successors had a number of the clan members executed, it was too late to eradicate their sorcery. Hartwig was told that until a chief named Ibanda came to power in the 1830s, the Kerewe had died natural deaths. Thereafter, his informant lamented, 'people died because someone had killed them.'

With occult powers no longer confined within the walls of the chief's palace, and as competition for trade goods turned villagers and even family members against one another, allegations of witchcraft took wing. Blaming a business rival when sickness or some other calamity entered a household not only provided a simple explanation; it also damaged the reputation of the accused. Some were forced to flee in fear of their lives, others had to deal with the suspicion and loss of trust of those they traded with. The historian Basil Davidson attributed the spread of witchcraft beliefs in nineteenth-century Africa to the 'growth of personal anxiety and alienation' brought about by the collapse of traditional structures and systems. In Ukerewe, sorcery quickly became part of everyday life.

The power of witchcraft shows no signs of weakening today. Many believe it is stronger than ever. Neither the spread of Christianity and Islam nor the increase in school enrolment and the arrival of television and the internet has loosened its hold. Witches – or people accused of being witches – inhabit every community. No misfortune occurs without someone pointing a finger; no success can be the result of merit alone. To counter the witches' power, witch doctors have proliferated. Cloth banners advertising their services are draped all over the archipelago. The tiniest market has stalls selling dull-coloured potions, bones, feathers and other animal parts. These medicines are available not just to experts but to anyone. One evening in my first week on the island, an old man in a bar, hearing me coughing over a ginger beer, had gone out to the street to buy me a porcupine quill. He told me – incorrectly, as it turned out – that if I held it over burning charcoal and inhaled the fumes, it would cure whatever was ailing me.

Just as in the nineteenth century, the renewed popularity of witchcraft is a response to crisis. After a brief period before the turn of the millennium when everything appeared to be going smoothly, the islands are again in a state of flux, and their inhabitants are turning once more to supernatural powers as an explanation for what is happening to them. Dina's divination business is booming as the islanders seek out the cause of the sudden downturn in their fortunes. There are rumours that the albino hunts on the mainland have reached Ukerewe as the trade in their body parts ratchets up. One night a woman living in our neighbourhood is murdered, her genitalia cut off and taken away for use in sorcery. Magical kidnappings are on the rise – Yohana tells us of a wedding on another island where a bride disappeared while receiving a gift from an aunt. She was taken by witches who had demanded that the aunt, a witch herself, hand over to them someone from her family. The girl is sometimes seen at night, Yohana says, but if you talk to her she vanishes again. For some, all this bewitchment proves too much – men and women driven mad by curses careen along the potholed streets of Nansio, their genitals and buttocks on display between the tears in their clothing as they peer into the gutter in search of food.

Sixteen

For the fishing boom – that dazzling efflorescence of commerce and possibility – has turned to bust. The feted *sangara*, which had usurped the chiefs of old as the guarantor of the islanders' well-being, is no longer able to fulfil its role as saviour. A perfect storm has hit Lake Victoria as the combined effects of predation and pollution have ravaged fish populations. Once a site of almost miraculous biodiversity and for so long Central Africa's greatest giver of life, the lake is now witnessing what one biologist has described as 'the first mass extinction of vertebrates that scientists have ever had the opportunity to observe.'

In 1832, William Forster Lloyd, a British mathematician and church minister, delivered a lecture in Oxford. In it, he wondered why cattle on commonly owned land are often puny compared with those kept in privately owned enclosures. He wondered, too, why the common land itself is always 'so bare-worn.' In answering himself, he demonstrated that common land is doomed to overuse, and that this destruction of a vital resource is a result not of human stupidity or greed, but of the rational calculations of cattle herders.

In an enclosed field, which has a finite quantity of grass, it is rational for a farmer to limit the number of cows in his herd: too many cows and the grass will run out and the cattle starve. Common land also has a finite quantity of grass, but on common land it is rational to keep increasing the size of your herd. For it is not just your herd that grazes on a common – there are other herds too. If you buy a new cow, what it eats will deplete the pasture, but the loss will be shared across all the herds. The total amount of grass consumed by your herd – and therefore the quantity of meat or milk your cattle produce – will increase if you add a cow to it, while if you don't add cows and other cowherds do, the latter will gain at your expense.

But your herd's increased productivity is short-lived. As in an enclosed field, more cows mean a more rapid depletion of the pasture. Eventually the pasture is exhausted and the cows grow punier. In a 1968 paper, the American ecologist Garrett Hardin demonstrated how Forster Lloyd's example applies not only to grazing land but to a wide range of environmental problems, from carbon emissions to acid rain to the dumping of waste in oceans and rivers. In the long-term, this "tragedy of the commons" condemns to destruction both the common resource and those using it. The common land will be stripped of grass, the cattle will run out of food, the herders will lose their herds. 'Each man,' Hardin wrote, 'is locked into a system that compels him to increase his herd without limit, in a world that is limited. Ruin is the destination toward which all men rush, each pursuing his own best interest.'

On the common waters of Lake Victoria, there were no limits to the number of individuals who could enter the fishing industry, and the fishermen and businessmen who came to the lake as the *sangara* boom took off had every incentive to acquire as many boats and catch as many fish as possible. In the mid-1980s, there were fewer than sixty thousand fishermen operating on the lake. By 2010 there were two hundred thousand. Two thousand new boats were launched onto the waters every year. As profits increased, more efficient technologies were introduced. Outboard motors were clamped to sterns, trawlers raked the lake bed, mesh sizes shrank. The number of monofilament gillnets – highly efficient nets which fish find harder to see than those with a thicker cord – increased from fifty-eight in 2004 to twelve thousand eight years later.

Nile perch is a large, powerful swimmer that has destroyed many a net, hook and boat, but the species has been unable to withstand the intensified efforts to catch it. Data collection by African governments is plagued by problems of financing, human capacity and corruption, and reliable official estimates of the extent of its decline are hard to come by. The Lake Victoria Fisheries Organisation has in some years produced data showing that the tonnage of Nile perch caught exceeded the tonnage of perch in the lake. Data gathered by zoologists is also contradictory. Some have found only a small decrease in the total annual catch size since the 1990s, others that it has plummeted.

Assessments of stocks of the fish are more consistent. They point to a decline of at least three-quarters in the tonnage of perch remaining in the lake. While the increased number of fishermen and the deployment of more efficient technology might for now have kept total catch sizes stable, they have caused a collapse in fish stocks that means the catch landed by each fisherman has shrunk by half.

The only perch to weather the storm are those that are too small for the nets. Most of the big fish have been harvested – the average weight of a caught *sangara* has fallen from fifty kilograms in the 1980s to less than ten today. The perch have altered biologically to cope with the onslaught: the size at which they reach sexual maturity has almost halved. But smaller individuals do not produce so many eggs, meaning that fewer perch will be born in future.

But still the fishing goes on. To catch the smaller perch, the fishermen use nets with smaller holes – many line their nets with mosquito nets donated by international aid agencies. Fish processing factories have successfully lobbied governments to slash the minimum permissible size at which a perch can be harvested, but as the size of caught fish has diminished, so has European and Asian demand. Most of the specimens on sale in the market in Mwanza are illegal, many not big enough to fill your plate. They are destined not for Israel, Japan and France but for the less affluent markets of Burundi, South Sudan and Congo.

The loss of its most lucrative customers cost the lake region nearly three billion dollars in the first decade of the millennium. Many of the processing factories have closed; most others are operating at half-capacity or less and have laid off thousands of workers. Fishermen have seen their incomes nosedive. Centurio tells me that during the boom, a small boat fishing off Kweru Mto could catch a hundred kilograms of Nile perch in a night. 'Today they are lucky to catch thirty kilos,' he sighs. Many of Ukerewe's fishermen have left their boats to rot on the beaches or sink in the shallows. Prostitutes, bereft of clients, are heading back to the mainland – one particularly beautiful girl from eastern Tanzania leaves when nobody can afford her eight-dollar fee. Joshua, who no longer has anything to paint as fishermen leave half-built the houses that were their lifetime's ambition, is one of numerous islanders who have turned in despair to drink.

Seventeen

The governments of Tanzania, Kenya and Uganda have made half-hearted efforts to arrest the slide. Trawlers were banned in 1991, although they continued to operate a decade later. The beach seines used by *kokoro* fishermen were banned in 1994, although the more affluent seine owners can bribe inspectors to turn a blind eye. Monofilament gillnets have also been outlawed, but their popularity continues to grow.

At the turn of the millennium the World Bank, which a few years previously had helped fuel the *sangara* boom by financing the establishment of the fish processing factories, joined in the scramble to rescue the industry. This time it provided funds to the Lake Victoria Environmental Management Project, which set up "Beach Management Units" around the lake. The BMUs were answerable to government fisheries departments. Their staff, which were supposed to include fishermen as well as local officials, were charged with vetting and controlling the number of new arrivals to the beaches, enforcing compliance with the new rules and arbitrating disputes. One thousand BMUs were established in the three countries around the lakeshore, and hopes were high that they would put a stop to illegal fishing.

The BMUs have failed. In 2006, Nile perch that were larger than the legal minimum catch size accounted for one in fifty of all Nile perch caught in the lake (to be legal a fish had to be at least half-a-metre long, a threshold which had shrunk from two metres at the beginning of the boom). Three years later, the proportion had fallen to one in a hundred. Revenues from illegal *sangara* sold within Africa came to dwarf those from the certified fish that were exported. Even after evolving to reach sexual maturity more quickly, most of the perch caught today are still too young to reproduce.

The BMUs were set up with no input from fishing

communities, which regard them as government agencies promoting government interests. Many of their members are boat owners or fish traders, who will lose out if they enforce their own rules. Fishing licenses, meanwhile, provide a vital revenue stream for cash-strapped district councils around the lake, and it is difficult for local officials to resist the temptation to register as many new fishermen as possible.

Hasani, I find out several weeks after our first meeting, is himself an illegal fisherman. His night-time sorties take him not to the open lake but to sheltered beaches onto which he and his men pull *kokoro* nets – beach seines. Hasani is at the bottom of the lake's fishing food chain; his target is *furu*, the cichlids whose rapid evolution made Lake Victoria such an ecological wonder. He sells them to Nile perch fishermen as bait. 'You need an outboard motor to catch *sangara*,' he says. 'The big ones are all in deep water. I don't have the capital for that.'

Hasani owns a wooden canoe. From his nightly expeditions in it he receives half the takings, with the remainder divided among his three-man crew. He has been in the business for a long time, and has earned the respect of his peers. Now and then I accompany him on walks or bike rides to other parts of the island, and when we reach a fishing camp he is always greeted warmly. He works at night because during daylight hours government patrol boats scour the beaches for *kokoro* fishermen like him. At night, he says, it's too dangerous for the patrols to come out – beach communities have been known to repel their approach with rocks or bows and arrows. The law enforcers brave the darkness only for a few weeks every year, and then only in convoys that are easy for the fishermen to spot.

One night he invites me to go out on the lake with him. At dusk we walk with the three men who will make up tonight's crew to the beach where he keeps his boat. As we pass along the narrow, dusty lanes between the closely packed houses, women call out greetings from yards illuminated by the flames of cooking fires. The women sit around the fires on the ground with their children, their menfolk either out on the lake themselves or, more commonly, no longer a part of their lives.

Two of the fishermen are over from Gozba, a *dagaa* fishing island in the west of the lake. They are taking advantage of the full moon to spend a week here with their families. The other man, Victor, older and wirier than his stocky colleagues, is a stalwart in Hasani's crew and can often be seen in the afternoons with him, passing around a joint or a cigarette while they repair their nets. Joshua has told us that he too will join us on the trip, but as we reach the lakeshore he is nowhere to be seen.

The canoe is hidden among bushes. A couple of years ago, Hasani tells me, it was stolen. Tipped off that it had been spotted in Mwanza, he went over on the ferry with a friend to take it back. The paddle home to Ukerewe took nine hours. I climb in and sit beside one of the men. Hasani takes his place behind us at the stern. There is no paddle for me – they say it would blister my hands. Whether this is because I am a feeble writer or because my white skin is too delicate I am not sure. Hasani's palms are as tough as old leather. Years of handling oars and ropes have left the brown skin crisscrossed with chalk-white lines.

We head out into the lake, three of them paddling vigorously while the older man bails water from the leaky hull with a cut-off jerrycan. Now and again Hasani stops paddling to point his torch at a beach. He is looking for an empty spot to fish from, and also checking for patrol boats that might be skulking in the shallows. We head southeast, skirting one side of Nansio Bay and deviating from our course only to avoid an inlet that is a popular haunt for hippos. Hasani shows me a dent where a hippo had bumped into the side of the canoe – the crew, ejected into the lake, were lucky the beast didn't attack. The weather is cool, a slight breeze rippling the full moon's reflection in the lake. Several of the beaches we pass are taken, their occupants dimly visible in the combined light of moon and torch. In the distance, to the west, a bank of thick black clouds does not escape the men's attention.

After half an hour we reach the lip of the bay. Turning out of it, we soon find a suitable beach to fish from. We jump into the shallows and haul the boat onto the pale sand. The strand is a hundred yards wide, sheltered on both sides by piles of rocks and stands of reeds. To the rear rises a boulder-strewn hill. A single small, gnarled tree stands in the middle of the beach, and the men tie around it the ropes that extend from each end of the *kokoro* net. On the hill above us crickets rub their wings, their whirr punctuated by the exuberant croak of frogs. Fireflies weave brilliant patterns as the dark clouds slide slowly towards the yellow moon. We have the whole beach to ourselves.

While the men are unloading the net from the boat we hear the splash of paddles. Another, larger canoe rounds the rocks and comes towards us. Joshua jumps out of it, drunk and laughing. He is followed by four other men with whom he has hitched a ride. The men are friends of Hasani's who have dropped in to help on their way back to Bezi, an islet to the south where they fish with long lines for *sangara*. They had come to Ukerewe to buy bait from Hasani and other suppliers. Joshua and I sit on the sand as two of the fishermen paddle out from the shore. They drape the net in a wide arc in the water, the apex perhaps half a mile out. On returning, they drag the boat back up onto the beach.

The men split into two lines, some thirty yards apart. Facing the lake in single file, their bare feet planted in the sand, they pick up the ropes. They are well lit by the moon – the night is light enough for me to write in my notebook. They wear shorts or rolled-up jeans, and long-sleeved shirts or jackets against the cool breeze. The foremost puller in each line stands in the water; the anchor man – after checking for safari ants, whose jaws are so strong that they are used in the bush to suture wounds – sits on the sand. As they begin their long tug-of-war with the lake, Hasani jogs between the lines, his extra pulling power making sure both sides of the net come in at the same speed. He heaves back, his calf muscles straining, heels sinking deeper into the sand. Below his back-to-front blue baseball cap, beads of sweat appear on his forehead. As he straightens to reach for another length of knotty cord, the simultaneous backward motion of the other pullers in his line keeps the rope taut.

Lightning flashes to the west as huge, flapping bats swoop overhead. The two lines of men edge closer together, tightening the trap around their unseen prey. They have been pulling for thirty minutes when the first squares of net, barely big enough to put your thumb through, appear above the quietly lapping waves. There is haste now in their pulling, which ensures the panicked fish have no time to escape. Hasani and one of the men from Gozba move forward to sit in the water between the ropes. As they reach for the stones that weight the bottom of the net, the black snails that carry the bilharzia parasite clack around their bare calves.

Twenty minutes later, the sac at the far end of the net finally comes into view. The men are more animated now, eager to inspect its contents. Joshua gets up to join in the pulling as with a final heave they drag it onto the beach. They stand over the sac, and Hasani shines his torch onto a mess of silvery fish. A dark shadow lands on a rock a little way out in the lake: a cormorant hoping for scraps. A black crab scuttles away from the pile, ignored. Among the mush of *furu* and *dagaa* are a single, foot-long Nile perch and a handful of baby perch. Without ceremony Hasani, the torch between his teeth, begins to sort the catch. He throws the perch into one bucket, to be sold in Nansio in the morning, and pours the *furu* into another. The *dagaa*, too small to be used as bait and insufficient in number for a meal, are thrown back into the water.

The Gozba men gather up the net and load it back into the

boat. One of them lights a joint, cradling it in his callused palm. Before he has finished smoking, we climb in and paddle off. Hasani continues the interminable sorting process on a net laid across the prow. I ask him if he enjoys what he does. 'God is great,' he replies. 'He gives us work and we do it. I have a family to provide for.'

We make for another beach a mile farther around the headland. The wind is getting up, the sky overhung with black clouds lit by regular lightning flashes. This beach is wide and rocky, and on one side there is another group of *kokoro* fishermen hauling in a net. The men who had brought Joshua in their boat raise a mast and run up a large white sail. Worried about the wind, they leave us and head for Bezi, the light from whose fires we can make out in the distance. If they had waited any longer, Hasani says, they would have been caught in the storm with the wind against them. 'It's going to be difficult enough for them already,' he adds.

With only four pullers left, the second net takes even longer to haul in. Flitting between the two ropes, Hasani complains that his men are lazy. He asks me if it would be possible to use a mechanical winch instead to pull in nets from the beach. 'A winch would do the job of two men, wouldn't it?' he says. His colleagues ignore his criticism, and discuss whether the stiffening breeze presages the first rain in months. Joshua wanders over to the other group of fishermen to help them sort their catch, while a teenage boy comes to our side of the beach to assist Hasani's crew.

The pulling proceeds calmly until the net comes into view. Only during the last few minutes is there any sense of urgency and, for me at least, excitement as I wait to see if they've caught anything substantial. But it isn't the big fish Hasani is after. He is content with the bucketful of shiny *furu* that each net yields, the by-catch of young *sangara* a bonus but not the focus of his operation. Although he knows why his method of fishing is banned, he doesn't agree that the perch will be wiped out if the intensity of the effort to catch them continues unchecked. 'The *sangara* produce thousands of young,' he says. 'If I catch a few of them, it's not going to make any difference. The politicians tell us we shouldn't fish like this, but there are no companies to work for and no government jobs. What else can we do? We don't have money to buy an outboard motor to go and fish in deep water, and even if we did, pirates would take our nets. I could pull a cart all day in town and earn five thousand shillings. That's enough for one person to live on, but not if he has six children and a wife. And the government wants us to send our kids to school – how can we do that if we don't even earn enough to eat?'

The moon has lost its race across the sky with the clouds and the breeze has become a wind. Normally the crew would pull in eight or ten nets a night, working until dawn when the patrols start, but Hasani is worried that if a storm gets up we will be marooned until morning and arrive back in Nansio too late to sell the catch. We paddle back to the first beach, nearer to home. In the two hours since we left it, its shallows will have refilled with fish. The ripples have swelled into small waves. The reeds rustle in the wind, the weaver bird nests that hang from them swaying like pendulums. Gazing at the thickening sky, the men discuss what to do. They decide there is time for one more net. They pull hard and fast for forty-five minutes. After they have hauled in a catch containing *furu*, *dagaa* and a catfish – once a popular fish for eating but now in danger of extinction – we head homeward.

They paddle with haste. There is thunder now, and big spots of rain spatter our heads. The night has gone dark, illuminated only by gigantic panels of lightning. Waves and gusts of wind buffet the little wooden canoe. We need to get back to the shelter of the bay, Hasani says. 'It's getting dangerous out here. If we'd stayed on the other beach we'd have been stuck.' Most of the four thousand people who drown in Lake Victoria every year are fishermen. Victor says he hopes the men who have left for Bezi are not in peril. We stick close to the shore, the men's paddling fast and urgent. The boat is letting in water and Joshua and I struggle to bail it out. The crew don't relax until we round the headland into the safety of the bay. It is three in the morning, too early for them to stop working even though the rain is now lashing. Hasani tells me they will fish for a few more hours, but since they will do so from the boat rather than the beach, they drop Joshua and me on shore. Hasani, ignoring my protests, hands me the foot-long perch to take to Ebru. We walk home in the driving rain as they paddle off into the darkness.

Eighteen

Most of Ukerewe's residents work for seven days a week on the lake or at their *shambas*, putting down their nets or hoes only for weddings or funerals. In Nansio, however, Sunday, for many, is a day of rest. It is spent either worshipping or drinking, or worshipping *and* drinking.

For young people on the island, the liquor of choice is either beer or sugarcane rum sold in sachets. Joshua mixes the two to achieve instant impact. The elders of the community have more eclectic tastes. Few drink beer, and most prefer home-brewed rum to the more expensive mass-produced version. For the elders who live in our neighbourhood, Sunday mornings offer a special treat. At around the time that most church services begin, they make their way to a compound a few yards down the road from our house, where two bulky middle-aged women in torn blouses and wraparound skirts sit in a bamboo shack stirring the contents of a large bucket. The bucket has been filled with *kindi*, a thick, white millet and maize porridge that has spent the previous two days fermenting in the women's houses. To serve the drink, which is by now strongly alcoholic, they squeeze it through a cloth into thermos flasks. In an adjoining shack, customers sitting at a low wooden table pour it from the flasks into plastic cups and get slowly, happily drunk. Mwalimu is a regular customer, as is an elderly woman who most people think is a witch. A few customers come from farther afield. One, a genial man in his late sixties named Kitina who visits the shack most Sundays, is a connoisseur of the island's traditional tipples. He lives in a village a few miles inland, and is one of Ukerewe's last practitioners of a dying craft.

In its heyday, banana beer was regarded as a great delicacy. It was used to propitiate ancestors, render tribute to chiefs or lubricate marriage negotiations. Aniceti Kitereza wrote about the tradition in his epic – and epically titled – Kikerewe novel, *Mr Myombekere and His Wife Bugonoka, Their Son Ntulanalwo and Daughter Bulihwali: The Story of an Ancient African Community*. In the story, Mr Myombekere's wife is accused by her new in-laws of being infertile. Unable to tolerate such slander, she leaves her husband and returns to live with her parents. Mr Myombekere, distraught, tries to get her back, but her father will agree only if his son-in-law brings him six large pots of banana beer as compensation for the slight to his family's honour.

To help him make the beer, Mr Myombekere enlists the assistance of a number of friends, but the task nevertheless takes over a week to complete. The process, described by Kitereza in painstaking detail, is meticulous. First, the young men collect fifty-three bunches of unripe bananas, which takes the better part of a day. Next they dig a pit. They dry the pit by burning grass, then line it with banana leaves. Onto the leaves they place the fruit, which they cover with banana tree branches, another layer of leaves and a layer of soil. Once the bananas are thoroughly buried, one of the men lifts the edge of this covering and applies a flame to the leaves, filling the pit with smoke. He replaces the lid and goes off with his friends to do other things for five days.

The novel was written in the 1940s and refers to a time many decades before that, but today Kitina follows a similar procedure. It had taken me months to track the old man down. After reading Kitereza's book I had asked around to find out if banana beer was still made on the island. Most young people I spoke to had never heard of it. A few of their elders had tried it in their youth – my mention of it brought dreamy looks to their eyes – but they told me that disease had decimated the banana crop in recent decades, and that since the modern preference was for mass-produced bottled beverages, those who knew how to make the beer no longer found brewing it to be a worthwhile use of their time. The knowledge had gradually died out, and there remained only two or three men on the island who still remembered the Kerewe recipe.

It was our friend Bebe who pointed me in the right direction. Bebe acted as a translator for the Canadian doctors during their visits to the island, but he spent most of his time working in his aunt's sundry goods store in Nansio market. One day he told us that a young man had come to town that morning from a village in the interior, hawking bottles of *mpahe*, as banana beer is known in Kikerewe. The man had told Bebe that it was his grandfather who brewed the beer, and Bebe, aware of my interest, had taken his phone number. I called to make an appointment to collect a few bottles, but the day before the meeting I received a text message saying his grandfather was otherwise engaged. I never heard from him again.

The trail seemed to have gone cold, until many weeks later Bebe called to inform me that another *mpahe* vendor, from a different village, had appeared in town. This one was on a bicycle, with ten plastic bottles strapped to his pannier. By the time I reached the market he had gone, but my frustration was alleviated when I saw that Bebe had bought one of the bottles himself.

We sat on a bench outside his aunt's shop to taste it. After placing two small glasses between us, he took out the mineral water bottle into which the elusive nectar had been poured. The liquid was brown and opaque. Bebe unscrewed the cap and we watched as the beer shot up out of the neck in a frothy swell and spilled in a torrent onto the ground. Again it seemed that our quest was to be thwarted.

By the time the foamy avalanche had abated there remained only a few drops in the bottle. We shared these dregs in sombre mood, the taste sweet and potent enough to make us wistful about what might have been. Bebe and the old man, Kitina, had exchanged phone numbers, but Kitina had told him that he seldom brews nowadays, and that with the dearth of bananas it was likely to be some time before he had any more to sell.

Nearly two months later, Bebe received a call. Kitina was planning a brewing session, and we were invited to go and see how he did it. The old man's village lies in sparse woodland a few miles west of Nansio. Its people are farmers rather than fishermen, and like our district it is well known for its witches. To reach the village we ask Rama to take us in his rickshaw. We leave early in the morning. It is cool and rainy, the dirt road muddy. As we bump in and out of the potholes, my head buffeting the metal frame of the vehicle's roof, the born-again Christian Rama tells Ebru and me that he disapproves of our plan for the day. 'The Lord does not allow us to touch alcoholic drinks,' he declares. 'We should drink soft drinks like Coke instead.' When I remind him that the Lord's son once turned water into wine, he laughs but is unpersuaded. He says he will drop us off and come later to pick us up, even though this will mean driving back to Nansio with no passengers, rather than staying to watch the artisan at work.

Kitina welcomes us into the yard at the rear of his windowless mud-brick house. He is tall and thin and sprightly, with a sparkle in his eyes and an easy warmth with strangers. He has lived in this village all his life, he says, and brought up thirteen children here. Banana beer is these days no more than a sideline for him; most of his meagre income is generated by selling the oranges, mangoes and passion fruit that grow on the trees in his garden. Pulling out wooden chairs for us, he points out the different trees. The ground beneath their branches is bare earth, softened only slightly by the rain. In the middle of the yard one of his adult daughters tends a cooking pot over a small fire – his wife is not mentioned, and Bebe guesses that the old man is probably a widower. The pot is filled to the brim with doughy cassava meal.

We listen to the trills of woodland kingfishers and the chirrups of weaver birds. The air is cool after the rain, the light less harsh than usual at this hour. A group of local children materialises, to gape at the foreigners. On the far side of the yard stands the tall, open-fronted shack that Kitina uses for brewing. 'I learned how to brew from my father,' he tells us. 'He learned from his father. After I pass on, I hope my nephew or one of my sons will take over from me. I'm teaching them how to do it, but I don't know if they'll keep it up.' Only a few of his children, he says, were able to complete their education. Most have migrated to the mainland in search of work.

In the absence of his sons he relies on his nephew, Pastore, to assist with the brewing process. Pastore arrives soon after us, a shy, well-built man in his twenties wearing a fake Real Madrid away shirt. After a lengthy greeting he beckons us to a field behind the shack. In a corner of the field is a low mound of earth: the banana pit. The fruits have been ripening here for six days. Pastore scrapes the earth aside with a hoe, revealing a rack of thick green banana tree branches. Beneath them the pit is piled high with buxom bunches of the newly yellowed fruit. Pastore shows us a clump of burnt mud and grass, and explains that he set this alight a few days ago to smoke the bananas (this artificial acceleration of the ripening assists the brewing process by turning starch into fermentable sugars).

One of the village boys removes the rack and jumps into the pit. He passes out the bananas. We each carry a bunch or two back to the brewing shack, which I notice through the gloom is decorated on its rear wall with a poster showing Tanzania's languid former president. On the floor of the tin-roofed structure lies an old dugout fishing canoe. We retake our seats outside, for once not having to worry about the sun's glare, and watch while Kitina and Pastore get to work.

After lining the canoe with sheaves of freshly scythed grass, they pluck the bananas from their stems and throw them in. 'In other places they peel the fruit first,' Kitina says, 'but in Ukerewe we leave the skins on. It makes pressing them harder work, but the best juice is in the skin.' His daughter brings him soap with a bowl of water and a small stone, and he kicks off his flip-flops and rolls up his trouser legs to wash and scrub his feet and calves. Taking up a long wooden pole for support, he steps into the dugout, which is now half-full with plump bananas, and begins to shuffle slowly along it.

In Aniceti Kitereza's novel, the treading process was undertaken by groups of four or five men, but today it is just Kitina. The old man moves down the dugout with short, careful steps, kneading the fruit under his heels and toes. As the bananas split open with the pressure, their sweet smell drifts out of the shack towards us. When he reaches the end of the canoe, he turns to retrace his steps. He holds the top of the pole by his shoulder – 'I have been known to fall in,' he explains with a smile. The bananas slowly yield to his weight, liquefying into a squelchy, pale-yellow pulp that oozes up between his toes.

Kitina has been making banana beer for nearly fifty years. These days, with demand for his product waning, he brews only three or four times a year. He produces around thirty litres each time and sells it for one thousand shillings a litre, less than half the price of a bottle of the *Kilimanjaro* beer we buy from Mama Neema's store. His clothes betray his financial straits – his once-yellow baseball cap is browned with sweat and dirt, and the heel of one of his rubber flip-flops has been sewn back on.

His daughter brings over a tray of spare bananas that she has salvaged from the pit. She curtseys, and pours water over our hands from a jug before we eat. The fruit is syrupy in its ripeness. Bees lured by the scent buzz around our heads. Looking over as he treads, Kitina tells us that the bananas of Ukerewe are sweeter than those found elsewhere in Central Africa. Nowadays, however, they are so scarce that he has to cycle to other villages to harvest them.

He slows his pace to press the more stubborn fruits between the balls of his feet. Bits of banana fleck his sinewy calves.

Almost an hour after the beginning of the process we see the first milky liquid spilling over his insteps. I ask if he is tired. He laughs. 'You people are used to machines so it looks tiring to you,' he says. 'For us it's normal.' While he treads he chats in Kikerewe to his daughter and Pastore. Neighbours pass by, some already drunk on *Konyagi*, a mass-produced sugarcane rum. An old man in a trilby tells us we must wait a week before we drink the *mpahe*. 'That's how we drank it in the old days,' he says with a wink. 'It's black by then, and so strong you won't be able to stand up.'

When the old man was young, *mpahe* would be taken to the chief's forest palace in tribute, carried in calabash gourds balanced on the brewers' heads. Now that the chief is in exile, the liquor's only remaining ceremonial role is to smooth marriage negotiations. Suitors take a few pots with them when they go to ask for their beloved's hand, and the men and women of the bride's household imbibe it while they discuss whether to allow the marriage and how big a dowry to demand. Even this custom is now dying out, however – Kitina says that today it's practised only in the remotest of the island's villages.

At length he steps out of the canoe. He and Pastore take up more sheaves of grass and lay them on top of the slough of mashed bananas. 'This is stage three,' he says. Stage three bears a strong resemblance to stage two, comprising many more laps of the dugout but with the grass acting as a strainer to force out more liquid. As the juice bubbles up and sloshes around the brewer's feet, the remaining banana pulp mixes with the grass to form a drying mat of turf (in the past this turf, once drained, would be eaten as a snack). After an hour Kitina bends to turn the mat over. He resumes his trudging, squeezing from it every last drop.

Some time later, when the turf has been wrung dry, Kitina and his nephew tilt the canoe to separate the liquid part of the mush from the solid. Pastore makes a sieve by stuffing grass into the cut-off neck of a jerrycan, and with a calabash gourd ladles the juice through it into a bucket. From another bucket he pours well-water onto the remaining sludge, and the treading begins again.

Other than the fruits themselves, banana beer's only ingredients are this well-water and a few grains of roasted millet, which are added later to speed fermentation. Kitina tips a little of the juice into his mouth from the calabash and pours us each a glass. I ask if he ever drinks the finished product himself. 'Sometimes when I deliver it to customers we sit and have a glass together,' he replies. 'Otherwise only if someone comes to ask to marry one of my daughters.'

For the final stage of the pressing process, Kitina uses a rack of wooden sticks tied together with string to extract the very last drops of liquid. He lays the rack over the top of the canoe and places on it a hunk of the banana and grass mixture. Taking up a second pole, and leaning on both as if on crutches, he stands on the clump of turf and kneads it under his feet. 'This is the hardest part,' he says, his body rising and falling above the rack. 'Walking up and down isn't tiring at all, but this is work. If you're not used to it, your heels and toes will be in pain for days afterwards.' A few drops of brown juice dribble down through the rack and into the dugout.

Each clump of hardening turf takes about five minutes to press with his clenching toes. When one is dry, with not a single drop remaining, he takes up another. There are seven or eight clumps. One of them will be used in a few weeks' time to smoke the next batch of buried bananas. In Aniceti Kitereza's book, the *mpahe* pressing takes a whole day. Kitina, with fewer bananas to crush, finishes in a little under five hours. He and Pastore stir the liquid in the canoe before pouring it and the juice from the bucket into two large clay pots where it will spend the next two days fermenting. Thinking that our visit is over, I ask if we should call Rama to collect us. Kitina is taken aback. He motions towards his daughter, who is still tending the pot on the fire. The air smells of frying onions and meat. 'Wait until we've eaten,' he says. 'It would be a shame on us if you came here as our guests and left without eating.'

A few days later I hear the bell of Kitina's bicycle outside our house. I go out to welcome him, and see the blue plastic bottle tops peeping up from his woven bamboo-leaf panniers. In Kitereza's novel, when Mr Myombekere delivers the fermented mpahe to his estranged wife's family, he is complimented in the traditional way. 'The dog who pressed this banana fruit into beer is a really great dog,' his satisfied father-in-law declares after drinking down a mouthful through a reed straw. The assembled guests are impressed enough with the brew to assent to the young lovers' reunification. They tuck into a meal of roast goat to celebrate.

Kitina sells me four bottles of the beer. We sit on chairs in the kitchen and I open the first bottle with care, loosening the cap a millimetre at a time to allow the frothing, breathing liquid to exhale without exploding. I pour us each a glass. The fermented brown liquor is flecked with black grains of millet. It is refreshing in the heat, no stronger than a regular lager. It tastes a little like a musty cider from rural England, but with an unmistakeable undercurrent of sweet, ripe banana. As we finish, and as Kitina climbs back onto his bicycle for the ride home, I remember the instructions of the old man in the trilby. I put aside one of the bottles, to be tackled when the beer inside turns black.

Nineteen

We would see Kitina from time to time in the ensuing months, either over a *kindi* in the women's shack of a Sunday morning or when he would stop by our house to greet us while passing on his bicycle. Gradually we developed a network of friends and acquaintances. On our strolls around Nansio we could stop by Bebe's aunt's store to chat to her or her nephew, or by the shop of an old Omani Muslim who had given me a glass of water one day when I was almost fainting in the heat. Often I would sit with Centurio in his new sundry goods store while he talked of the venality of the government and of the opposition party of which he was a member. Business, he said, was terrible. 'Mr Mark is my best customer,' he told me one afternoon with a mournful smile. The three bottles of water I bought from him most days were keeping him afloat.

Other people we had given business to also became friends. The cobbler who sat in the street near the island's juice bar, who had once sewn together the sole of my old sandals with string for a couple of cents, would wave a greeting whenever we passed. Rama would call us over to his rickshaw to talk about Jesus while he waited for customers. Zadock, the town's most renowned handyman, who in repairing the broken hinge of my glasses one day had left one of the lenses covered with superglue, would get up from his shack when he saw us to spend a few minutes shooting the breeze. And Nitoni, the Sukuma porter who had helped us with our luggage when we first arrived, would stop us to complain of the islanders' attitude to outsiders. 'They think we take their jobs,' he would say as a frown crumpled his bony forehead. 'They don't treat us well.'

On previous trips around Africa we had tended to move quickly between stops. In a half-year stint in West Africa we had spent no more than five or six weeks in a single place. Living for a few months in a small town in South Africa, we had stayed in a compound for expatriates and had had only limited interaction with local people outside the health research centre where we were working. Although we had made friends in these places – it would be difficult not to in Africa – the friendships had been a little rushed, the pace of their development unnatural.

In Ukerewe, on the other hand, we had a surplus of time. There was little to do but get to know the neighbours, and we had two years in which to do so. We could postpone days out and stay at home absorbing our surroundings instead. There was no hurry to work out which child belonged to which parent or which husband to which wife, nor to learn about all the different fishing techniques or farming practices. There was time to observe how the children changed as they grew up, and to discern the shifting relationships between the adults of the community. We saw the seasons – the mango rains late in the year, which would be remembered months later in the succulent fruits the children harvested from the tree outside our house; the dry season whose prolongation was the despair of farmers; and the blessed long rains, these days so often curtailed. Slowly, too, the vast gulf that had separated us from the islanders – a gulf so evident on the ferry that had brought us here and in the shouts of "Mzungu" that we continued to field whenever we left our neighbourhood – began to narrow.

Adjusting to life on the island often required us to question our own convictions. One morning early in our stay I was sitting inside writing when I saw Hasani climb into the branches of a spindly tree that towered over Baraka's house. He had borrowed a saw and was cutting off every limb he could reach. When he descended, stripped to the waist and gleaming with sweat, he began to saw at the base of the trunk. Remembering what Mabiba had told me about the deforestation of the island, and in general preferring trees to be left vertical, I went out to ask what he was doing. I felt indignant, but restrained myself and put the question politely. A group of children were sitting watching him, and they were now watching me too. Hasani, whom I didn't yet know well and whose smile as I approached vanished as soon as I began to speak, looked at me levelly. His family needed firewood, he said, and he had bought the tree from Baraka, on whose land it stood. His firm gaze made it obvious that he knew why I'd rushed outside, and equally obvious that his family's ability to cook food and to stay warm during the cool nights of the mango rains was more important than allaying my bourgeois Western angst. 'Tupo,' he said after a while. This phrase's literal meaning of "we are here" is normally used to encourage visitors to sit for a while, but in this case it seemed to mean "you can stay or go as you please". The conversation was over, and as I retreated he bent to finish the job.

For a day or two after the incident I kept my distance, embarrassed, but Hasani, whose understanding of my position was more nuanced than mine had been of his, quickly forgot about it. Even after we had lived on the island for two years we would still be seen as outsiders. The "Mzungu" shouts on our walks to and from town would never cease, and we remained an object of fascination to islanders who came across us for the first time. Those who got to know us, on the other hand – our neighbours, the villagers of Kabuhinzi, our friends in Nansio – came to treat us more naturally. They would greet us as they would each other, without the shock or amusement of old, and would defend us against hecklers. 'One must not run through a country,' as the explorer Stanley wrote, 'but give the people time to become acquainted with you and let their worst fears subside.'

The extent to which Stanley lived up to his dictum is disputed by historians, but our presence on Ukerewe helped open minds other than our own. Before we arrived on the island, Joshua had had little to do with Hasani and his friends. Having received a good education in the metropolis of Dar es Salaam he saw himself as a sophisticate. He spoke English, wore fashionable jeans and T-shirts, and had had a number of wealthy girlfriends. The fishermen, who wore cast-off European clothing and in many cases couldn't read or write, he regarded as his inferiors. Unlike the newly successful businessman Masondole, who studiously ignored all our neighbours when he came to check on the house, Joshua would at least spare them a greeting of a morning. But when the foreigner Gloria landed in the community with her convention-defying leggings, her frequent visits to the mainland and her disdain for the local hicks, Joshua enthusiastically became her only friend.

As an outsider, my awareness of these class divides was weak – other than a few successful entrepreneurs like Masondole and Mabiba, it seemed to me that everyone here was struggling to put food on the table. Hasani and Joshua's finances were equally straitened, but when in the early days I would ask Joshua to translate Hasani's words for me, he would interject asides about his neighbour's ignorance. Whether Hasani was discussing the benefits of having as many children as possible, or the pointlessness of taking a poorly Magesa to the government hospital where 'they will just put him on a drip of water and charge us thousands of shillings for it,' Joshua would invariably add with a smile that 'he doesn't understand, he's not educated.'

By the time we left the island, Joshua and Hasani had become good friends. Whether this was because of our example or because Joshua had been humbled by two years of unemployment I am not sure – he insisted it was the former – but by the end of our stay I would often see them chatting in front of Hasani's house, and Joshua would come over and join in our conversations even though by then I had no need of a translator. Hasani also took Joshua into the circle of those he occasionally helped out, giving him a little cash or a loan when he had no money to buy food. Cristina was also in this circle, as were most current or former members of Hasani's fishing crew.

Our influence on our younger friends was not always appreciated. Our relationship with Mabiba cooled after a couple of months, at least in part because he disapproved of our effect on Neema. Wearing trousers was one thing, but once her attendance at Winners' Chapel declined the blame fell on us. Neema told us that she had cut down on her churchgoing because the services were too long and because her absence from home late into the evening had been causing problems with her mother and brother. But from Mabiba's frostiness towards us in the wake of her decision, it was clear that he thought we were behind it. The pastor told Neema that bad things would happen to her if she didn't go to church. 'Maybe when he tells her that,' Ebru mused, 'she says Mark and Ebru never go to church and they're the best-off people on the island.'

In our first days on Ukerewe we had clung to people like Mabiba and Gloria for support. In an environment that was so alien to us, those who spoke English and knew the world beyond the lake offered both a link to the familiar and practical connections to the cities of the mainland in case of a crisis. But as each of these props dropped away we were left to fend for ourselves. When travelling around a country you can move on if there are difficulties, but being forced to stay in a place for many months gives you no choice but to find strength in your own resources. In West Africa I had succumbed to the stresses we had faced on our journey – Ebru, more resilient, had helped me through the breakdown I experienced there. But here, as the weeks passed, I could feel my mind growing stronger. As we settled into our new life I became less irritated by hustlers, less irked by hecklers shouting "white man" or "give me money", and less stressed by the little annoyances that had slowly worn me down in the western part of the continent. From those around me I learned to be more patient in the face of discomfort and delays. I got used to power and water cuts, even to the extent of feeling virtuous to be enduring such hardships. A serious setback – an illness or a robbery, an argument or a fight – would no longer put me off the whole island and prompt me to flee to safer shores. Quite quickly the sensation developed – an almost physical sensation – of being at home in these surroundings, and able to cope with whatever they threw at me.

A further unexpected benefit of our long stay was the opportunity to learn more about the lives of women. In West Africa we had met a few women in passing, but it is more often men who accost you in the street, who frequent the bars and restaurants, who drive minibuses and motorbike taxis, and who have the confidence to strike up a conversation. Most women are either too busy to waste time chatting to foreigners or too worried by what their families and friends will think.

In Ukerewe, too, the women of our neighbourhood kept their distance at first. On one occasion Lilian, carrying a bucket of maize from her *shamba* to be milled, had found herself on the same path as Ebru and me. She looked embarrassed to be walking with us, and laughed a little too loudly as other women called out to her from their yards. We later realised that a fear of gossip was the reason for her shyness. Hasani is an enlightened man by Ukerewe standards – he helps out with household chores and asks his wife's opinion on business matters – but Lilian had worried that reports of her walking into town with a strange man, even with Ebru present, might filter back to her husband.

As time passed, however, and as Hasani came to trust us, she grew friendlier, and she and Ebru would eventually become close. After a few months she had relaxed enough to confide in her new friend about the problems faced by women on the island. Since Ebru was too busy working to learn much Swahili and my own command of the language was now quite strong, I would join them to help with translation.

Lilian has four surviving children. As well as Ali and

The Saviour Fish

Magesa, fathered by Hasani, she has a son and a daughter who are the products of a previous relationship, from before she moved to the lake from her village near the Kenyan border. In her household she also looks after Saidi, Hasani's son from a previous marriage; Rama, who they took in after his father, Hasani's brother, died; and Mase, Lilian's nine-year-old niece whose mother recently passed away.

Hasani would like at least ten children. Having large families is a symbol of virility and success, but Hasani has another motivation. 'Children here are capital,' he tells me one afternoon as he sits on the ground mending a net. 'They help you around the house and in the *shamba*, and if you have many children there is more chance that one of them will be successful and help the whole family to have a better life.'

Complications while giving birth to Magesa a couple of years ago mean Lilian is no longer able to reproduce, so Hasani has begun an affair with a woman who lives down the road towards the lake. The woman has given birth to a baby son, whom Hasani supports and whose visits to be played with by his father and half-siblings Lilian has no choice but to tolerate. She tells Ebru of her unhappiness with the situation, and laments the unfairness of it being deemed reasonable for married men to take other women while their wives must remain monogamous. Hasani is sympathetic about her condition, she says, but it has nevertheless altered her status in the relationship.

The importance of producing children leads some women to unusual lengths. Late one night after the neighbourhood had gone quiet, Joshua rapped on our metal gate asking to be let in. His hushed voice was panicky, and he perched nervously on the edge of the sofa as he told us what had happened. A year ago, he said, he had met and seduced a girl in a bar. She had told him she was single, and it was only later that he found out she had a husband, a local businessman. The husband, Joshua said, 'couldn't get her pregnant,' but Joshua could, and a few months ago she had given birth to a daughter.

Joshua's relationship with the woman had endured no longer than it took to impregnate her, and he had been happy for the married couple to take care of the baby they'd longed for without making any demands on him. But that afternoon the husband had come round to Joshua's house. He told Joshua that for several days the baby had been crying incessantly whenever he was at home. She would begin wailing as he walked in the door in the evening and continue until he left for work the following morning. To find out why, he had taken the baby to see a witch doctor. There he had been told, to his shock, that he was not the child's father. He went home and forced his wife to tell him who the culprit was. 'If the baby doesn't stop crying,' he promised Joshua after storming round to his house in a rage, 'you will die.' Joshua was terrified – he told us that the man would kill him not with his own hands but with witchcraft. 'I'm going to Mwanza tomorrow,' he said. 'I might not come back. You don't believe these things because you don't know the environment. Ukerewe is different – the witches here are too strong. I'm afraid.'

The number of chores women like Lilian carry out every day is dizzying. Rising at dawn, she dresses the younger children and lights the fire in the yard to cook their morning cup of *uji* or tea. When Ali and Magesa emerge from the fenced-round pit dug into the ground that is the family's toilet, she cleans them with water. Hasani and his crew make their own tea over the same fire when they come back from fishing, by which time Lilian, having washed the tin cups and pan, is on her way to the lake for the first of what might be half a dozen daily visits. At the lakeshore she washes a pile of clothes and collects water for the day in a bucket. Tatu, her daughter, accompanies her on one or two of these trips before leaving for school. The buckets they carry back on their heads hold eighteen litres of water, almost one-third of Lilian's body weight and perhaps two-fifths of Tatu's. The weight of the water will eventually damage their spines as well as causing daily neck and back pain, and they will be significantly shorter when they are old than they are now. In our second year on the island, Tatu would be relieved of water-carrying duties when she contracted spinal tuberculosis, a dangerous disease which could have led to paralysis if she hadn't promptly begun a six-month course of treatment. Although Saidi and Rama would take up some of the slack, Tatu's absence increased the burden on Lilian.

After the early morning chores are completed by hanging the washed clothes out to dry, Lilian heads for her *shamba*, a three-mile walk away along the southern shore of the island. After a few hours of ploughing, planting, gathering firewood or weeding, each undertaken using either hand-held tools or her bare hands, she returns home. If it's harvest time she will take her grain to the mill or spend an hour smashing beanstalks on the ground to separate the pulses from the leaves. Those of her children who have returned from school will join her in the subsequent sifting process.

Lunch is not a regular occurrence, but when the farming has been good there is *ugali* made from the corn she has grown, and perhaps a few *dagaa* from Hasani's by-catch as seasoning. The meal is cooked and eaten indoors – although the smoke from the charcoal-fed stove puts the family at risk of respiratory and heart problems as well as various cancers, eating inside averts the danger that prying eyes will envy their good fortune and put a curse on them.

Lilian's work, like that of most women here, is not limited to the household and the *shamba*. She also has a side business plaiting neighbours' hair. She spends the middle part of the afternoon on a little stool in the yard with a customer sitting on the ground between her legs. The braiding process is slow and sociable – other women drop by to watch and chat or to wait their turn – and it offers Lilian respite from the whirl of more physical tasks. For each head of hair she braids she earns five hundred shillings, enough to buy a couple of hundred grams of rice.

One of Ebru's students at the teacher training college, a confident woman from the Mount Kilimanjaro region whose husband Nurdin takes Ebru to work every day in his taxi, is of the opinion that the men of Ukerewe are lazy good-for-nothings. They loaf around all day, she says, while the women do all the work. 'Some of them fish, but most of them just loiter. It's always the women who find food for their families.'

Lilian and her friends seldom let up in the work they do at home and in the fields. But it seems to me that Hasani and many other male islanders also work more or less constantly. If he isn't out on the lake fishing – a gruelling occupation, especially for a *kokoro* fisherman – Hasani is mending nets or helping Lilian at the *shamba*. Mwalimu, although disabled and well past what would be retirement age if Tanzania had such a thing, sits for hours under his tree, long after the main classes of the day have finished, giving extra tuition to children who are falling behind. Centurio works in his shop from dawn until just after dusk, resting only on Sunday mornings when he goes to church. The drivers Nurdin and Rama spend at least twelve hours a day, seven days a week, waiting for rides.

Research by the World Bank suggests that women in developing countries work an average of fifty minutes more than men each day, if unpaid work is included. In developed countries the difference is thirty minutes. In Africa as a whole, women carry out about forty per cent of agricultural work, and in Tanzania slightly above fifty per cent. But while Ebru's student may be slightly underestimating some men's contribution, she is right that women in Africa are discriminated against in the labour market. Across the continent, men are significantly more likely to be in paid employment than women, and they earn more money for doing the same work. This financial advantage combines with cultural norms to give them a dominant position in their households. In most families men control the money, have the last word in important decisions, and are freer than their wives to have extramarital affairs and to go out enjoying themselves with friends.

When this imbalance tilts in the opposite direction, it causes ribaldry. One of our neighbours, a pale-skinned man with wiry black hair, is of Arab descent (his ancestors would have come here from the coast to trade in slaves or skins or ivory). Known as *Mwarabu*, The Arab, he is married to a Tanzanian. Such a union would usually make for a highly unequal partnership, with the wife expected to carry out all domestic and farming tasks and the husband able to relax on coming home from work and at weekends. But in this case the roles are reversed. The Arab works at the ferry dock, doling out tickets and sweeping. After toiling all day for a meagre salary, when he comes home he must sweep the house, fetch water from the lake, cook dinner and look after his children. As his wife sits back and chats with friends while he labours, the men of the neighbourhood look on with amused pity. Some believe that if he refuses to work, his wife, a large woman grown fat on leisure, will beat him. Others attribute his servitude to witchcraft – only by poisoning his food with secret medicine, they muse, could a woman attain such control over a man.

Twenty

Joshua proves to be a rich source of witchcraft stories. The problem with the businessman had blown over once the baby recovered from whatever was ailing her, and he and his wife had resumed rearing the little girl as if Joshua – and the witch doctor's diagnosis – had never existed. But although he is well-educated by Tanzanian standards, and although his religious faith is unswerving, Joshua remains convinced of the power of the occult, and lives in constant fear of its effects.

He is aware, too, of foreigners' fascination with sorcery. This is sometimes criticised by commentators on Africa for exoticising the continent and making it look backward (an interest in Islam or Christianity, which also rely to a great extent on the miraculous, escapes such opprobrium). But on Ukerewe, witchcraft is such an integral part of daily life that it would be perverse not to pay heed to it. Some of my most absorbing hours are spent listening to Joshua's perspective on the phenomenon.

He takes pleasure in shocking me with its possibilities. One afternoon he sits on our step and tells me about crocodiles. On one of the islands of the archipelago, he begins, there is a tree which leans out over a beach. Normally its dead leaves fall onto the sand and nothing unusual happens. But now and then, when the wind is blowing in the right direction, a leaf falls into the lake, metamorphoses into a crocodile and glides away.

The sunlight filtering through the mango tree is bright and clear. The children are taking turns to hurtle around the block on a bicycle one of their parents has rented for the day. Riding in tandem with one child on the seat and another on the crossbar or handlebars, they shout at the top of their voices as they weave among the line of girls in knee-length skirts who are trooping to the lake with buckets. The fishermen opposite snooze on their piled-up nets, oblivious to the mayhem.

There are people, too, Joshua continues, who have the power to create these dangerous beasts. They take up a rope and fling it into the lake. After a few seconds the rope turns into a crocodile and swims off. The most powerful witches can harness crocodiles to fetch absconding debtors or faithless lovers. 'You can be drinking a glass of water,' Joshua says, as a posse of small children huddles around our legs to listen to the alien language, 'and suddenly the glass turns into a lake and a crocodile lunges out of it and swallows you.' The reptile bears you in its stomach back to where the witch is waiting, and regurgitates you, alive, to meet your fate.

Animals play a part in many witchcraft stories. An aunt of Joshua's was once seen riding a cow at night, naked. In this she was following an ancient tradition. The local historian Bahitwa told Gerald Hartwig in the 1960s of a type of witch known as an *omuzinilizi*. According to Hartwig, this is a character 'of considerable antiquity ... who has animal or bird familiars, convenes nakedly at night with others of his kind, and has the power to make himself or herself invisible.' Similar witches, who are more of a social nuisance than a threat to life, have been found among the Tswana people of modern Botswana, thousands of miles to the south, but the Ukerewe *omuzinilizi* were distinguished by their 'particular affinity for riding other people's cattle during nocturnal ventures.'

Witchcraft can be used for good as well as evil. When we first arrived in Ukerewe we had had to decide whether to appoint a security guard for our house. All of Ebru's colleagues in other parts of Tanzania had guards, which were paid for by the employer, and since as the only white people on the island we would be highly visible to criminals, we were advised to give the idea strong consideration. After a few weeks we had decided against it. Having a guard would have required putting a fence around the house, which would have been an even greater barrier between us and our neighbours than were our metal gate, our weak grasp of the language and the gulf in our backgrounds. When we left the house during our first year for a Christmas visit to Burundi and Rwanda, we expected to discover on our return that it had been burgled. Thieves, we supposed, would assume it contained rich pickings; the metal bars on the gate were sufficiently widely spaced to allow a child to squeeze through; and neither the windows nor the front door were robust enough to resist a determined shove. When we arrived back from the trip to find the house unbreached, we concluded with satisfaction that our most effective protection against intruders was the watchfulness of our neighbours.

Joshua, however, has a different explanation for our immunity to misfortune. As two of the wealthiest people on the island, we were an obvious target for the curses of envious neighbours and the powerful witches for whom our district was notorious. That in two years we suffered none of theft, fire, illness or impoverishment, therefore, could only be due to sorcery. The mother of our landlord Masondole was a formidable witch, famous across the archipelago. It was because of her diabolic powers, Joshua reports, that her son suddenly came into the money that he invested in building our house. When he laid the foundation stones, he would have buried among them a potion prepared by his mother. This potion – a powder made of tree bark or ground-up leaves wrapped in a cloth purse – would protect the house and those living in it against the many who would try to cause them harm.

A few months before the end of our stay, Masondole's mother died. I asked Joshua if her spell would continue to shield us from harm. He nodded. 'She was a very big witch,' he said. 'Her medicines are very strong.'

Along with time spent with the children, these afternoon conversations with our neighbours would become the most treasured moments of my time on Ukerewe. When I'd heard we were to be posted to the island I had worried about the prospect of spending swathes of time alone, and that the minor nervous breakdown I'd suffered in West Africa might recur. But in Ukerewe it is impossible to feel lonely. Even if it is only a brief visit from a neighbour, to make sure I have survived the night or to let me know that they are still around and interested in my friendship, seldom does an hour go by without human contact. Humans are humans because of other humans, goes a Bantu saying, and as our weeks on the island stretched into months this closeness between people struck me ever more strongly. In West Africa, where we had spent most of our time in towns and cities, this hadn't been so noticeable – people there, uprooted from their village homes, were more atomised, and competition for jobs, land and food created friction between them. But after leaving rural Tanzania and returning to Europe, I would often feel a heavy loneliness, a sense of loss, in environments in which I hadn't previously noticed my solitude.

The closeness between the children of Ukerewe is also remarkable to a European observer. As soon as they are able to crawl, they spend the entire day surrounded by other children. As well as multiple brothers and sisters, there are neighbours, cousins, more distant relatives and sometimes just other children who happen to be passing through the neighbourhood and are enlisted to join in games or share in a discovery. There are dozens of children to spend time with – they need never be on their own. And they interact not just with children of the same age but of all ages. On our step, Ali, aged three, Devidi, aged five, and Zebe, aged seven, will sit with the young teenagers Saidi and Tatu, and with pre-teen Pascali and Peter. Three-year-old Lisa often comes over too, making her elders laugh with her hallucinatory stories. She sometimes brings her baby sister Vei over on her back, and the others play with her like doting parents. Nobody is turned away; anyone who wants to join in is integrated seamlessly into whatever activity the others are engaged in.

In difficult times, this human contact is a vital resource for the islanders. Early one morning we are woken by a series of loud wails from the direction of Mwalimu's school under the tree. We look out to see Mazigo's mother – Joshua's aunt – standing in front of her house behind the school, keening and weeping with her hands pressed to her temples. Her young sons Mazigo and Katondo stand nearby, a look of incomprehension on their faces. Her two older daughters sit blank-faced on stools with Anita and Rosa, younger girls left with the family by destitute relatives. We dress hastily and as we open the front door bump into Joshua. His uncle Baraka, he tells us, has died during the night. Baraka, disabled by his bloated stomach and by his gradually worsening illness, had for many months been confined to the chair outside his house. A few weeks ago he had been transferred to Nansio Hospital. Joshua had taken me one day to see him. He had been nothing more than a sack of bones, barely able to raise a whisper, but was grateful, nonetheless, that we had made the effort to visit.

Baraka's death is ascribed by most people in the neighbourhood to witchcraft. For years he had made a living fishing for Nile perch, but as the fishing became more difficult and his brood of children expanded, it became impossible to make ends meet. When he needed a new net, he stole one from another fisherman. His crime was discovered and a witch was paid to curse him. Within months his health had deteriorated to the point where he was unable to get up from his chair.

Baraka's family turned to witch doctors for an antidote to the curse. Only when his stomach swelled to late-pregnancy proportions while he simultaneously shed stones in weight did they resort to what passes on the island for modern medicine. The failure of the hospital to cure him had confirmed their original suspicions. 'People try witch doctors first,' the scientific Centurio had observed during one of our afternoon chats in his shop, 'but when the illness gets really bad they go to hospital.

Then when they die, everybody thinks the hospital killed them.' With their own failures forgotten, witch doctors continue to thrive.

Baraka's symptoms – a distended abdomen, mental disorientation and constant drowsiness (he spent much of his time asleep) – suggest bilharzia as an alternative explanation for his plight. This disease, also known as schistosomiasis, is rife around Lake Victoria. The black freshwater snails which carry the bilharzia parasite are a common sight floating near the beaches, and anyone who washes, swims or fishes in the lake is at risk of infection. The snails release larva into the water, which burrows through human skin and grows into half inch-long worms. The worms' eggs pass back into the lake in urine and faeces. When they hatch, they find a snail to inhabit and the cycle begins again.

The worms can live in the human body for decades – if the disease goes untreated, they can cause liver failure and a dangerous accumulation of fluid in the abdomen. Treatment is inexpensive, but the symptoms of the acute stage of bilharzia – stomach ache, a cough, fatigue and fever – are not severe by the standards of tropical Africa, and they abate after a few weeks even as the worms remain in the body. Many islanders are infected repeatedly – as well as its multiple other roles, the lake is used as a toilet, and for those who don't live near a well there is no cleaner water source. Most families are ignorant of the long-term risks posed by the disease, and few see medication for a non-urgent condition as a worthwhile use of scarce funds.

Joshua takes us over to commiserate with his aunt. She acknowledges us briefly before continuing her lamentations. Soon she is joined in her anguish by Mwalimu's wife. Other women begin their own supportive howls as they near the bereaved house. With each new arrival, the wailing of those already there briefly intensifies. As the number of mourners grows, the young children of the neighbourhood – Ali, Magesa,

Lisa and the rest – look on in troubled fascination.

Muslims here are normally buried within hours of death, but Baraka's wife can't afford to have the body brought home from the hospital. Joshua would tell us this a few days later, when the time came for us and other neighbours to give what we could to help the deceased's family. The delay allows time for more visitors to arrive, from Ukerewe itself and on ferries from other islands and from the lakeshore. Relatives, neighbours, passing strangers and old friends come by to pay their respects. To show their solidarity, it is enough simply to sit outside the house with the family for as many hours – or in most cases days – as they can spare. Although a gentle and popular man, whom passers-by would always stop to greet, Baraka was no eminent personage. Yet by the afternoon there are at least eighty people milling about in the shade of the trees.

Guests bring with them whatever they can afford. Funerals can be an expensive business in Africa, but this family barely has the means to feed itself, much less dozens of long-term guests. Some visitors bring money, others sacks of rice or beans from their *shambas* or tin plates piled high with *ugali*. The very poorest bring a couple of sticks of firewood. With so many people providing support merely by being there, the mood gradually lightens. Men play cards, the rumble of chatter is unceasing, and as the day wears on the talk begins to be punctuated by laughter. Seifu, Baraka's eldest son, joins in a card game. Mazigo sits quietly while his brother Katondo, too young to take in what has happened, goes off to play. The eldest daughters bring out chairs and a bed for guests to sit on, and busy themselves sweeping the space in front of the house. Their mother retreats inside, to welcome visitors who must pay their respects in private before joining the throng.

At night, the houses around the grassy patch between Baraka's house and ours fill with guests. Men and boys for whom there is no room sleep on rattan mats outside, withdrawing into a nearby cattle kraal when it rains. Two young women, cousins of Joshua's from a village in the west of the island, settle down to sleep on our veranda. Joshua, Mazigo and Katondo take the double bed in our spare room, bringing a smile to Mazigo's face for the first time that day.

By the following afternoon there are three hundred people on the patch of grass. Baraka's body is brought home in a Land Rover emblazoned with the logo of the Party of the Revolution. A bell is rung to announce the imminent burial. Everybody stands up while Dickson, a Christian, reads a text from the Bible. A few men retrieve the body from the back seat of the car. It is wrapped in a white shroud. They lift it with ease and carry it away along the road that skirts the lakeshore. The women and most of the children stay behind.

The local graveyard, which lies a few yards from the glittering lake, looks like a patch of overgrown wasteland. Most of the graves are unmarked and covered by long grass and scrub. Only a few bear crude wooden crosses or iron crescents. Baraka's grave has already been dug, by Joshua and some of his friends. We stand around it, the sun's rays pressing down on our heads. A blue sheet is held over the pit and rippled like waves as the body is tipped into the arms of two waiting gravediggers. Onlookers, among them the dead man's son Seifu, throw in sticks and leaves before the diggers fill the pit with earth. An elderly imam in a skullcap delivers a brief sermon, urging Muslims to go to the mosque and Christians to church, so that we will remember why we have been put here. There is more to life, he tells us, than Premier League football and mobile phones.

Back at the wake that evening, a strip-light is suspended from a tree and attached by a long wire to a plug socket in our house. The family's makeshift cooking shack is abuzz with activity. Everybody mucks in with the cooking, the serving of food and the washing up. Beans bubble in huge aluminium pots stirred with wooden canoe paddles. Groups of children sit on the ground waiting for teenage boys to pour water on their hands and bring them a dollop of *ugali* to share. New arrivals who break out into wails – women in brightly coloured headscarves and matching dresses who have come in on the afternoon ferry from the mainland – are ignored until they have paid their respects inside the house and emerged again to join the feast. The hum of chatter competes with the crickets' eternal trill.

Sitting on the ground among them, I tell Joshua that I admire the camaraderie that so many people are showing Baraka's family, and that I am surprised to hear the sound of laughter among all the talk. 'There's no way out,' he replies. 'He can't come back. This is our last time together.' When I tell him that it's rare in England for so many neighbours to spend so much time with the bereaved he looks at me in disbelief. As my words sink in he shakes his head and clicks his tongue, as if I have infringed some terrible taboo.

A week after Baraka's death, there are still people arriving to pay their respects, although the permanent mourners are down to a hard core of a few dozen (the last guests will finally leave on the tenth day, although many will come back three weeks later for the forty-day anniversary). That night Mwalimu, who has lost his best friend as well as his brother, buys a jerrycan of moonshine made by his wife's sister. A few of us sit on stools on the patch of grass in the darkness, drinking it from plastic cups.

Tonight the distribution of Baraka's property is to be decided. Other than the one-room house which will be left to his wife and young children, this amounts to a cow, half a wooden fishing canoe and half a fishing net. These last two possessions he had owned in partnership with another neighbour, Masusu, who lives on the other side of the dirt road. Before Baraka's illness the two men had fished together for Nile perch, paddling out at night into the deep waters of the lake and sleeping in the boat until the time came to gather in the nets in the morning. Masusu is normally a cheery fellow with a ready smile, who whenever he passes our house greets me in Kikerewe in a vain attempt to teach me the language. But his friend's death has hit him hard and he has spent the last few days drunk.

The adult male members of the extended family take turns to pronounce their views on what should be done. Each of them stands to give his opinion – Mwalimu, Dickson, a couple of other neighbours and a few men who have come from afar to be here. Baraka's wife sits to one side with her sisters-in-law and listens. After every man has spoken there is a patient discussion of the options. Eventually it is decided that Baraka's property will be sold off and shared between his ten children, with his wife looking after the part allocated to those too young to use it. Masusu, who these days fishes with his teenage nephew, is too upset to give an opinion.

Twenty-One

Those islanders who blame Baraka's death on a curse overlook a more likely culprit: the fishing industry. The latter's decline meant that Baraka couldn't afford the treatment that might have cured his illness before it reached such a dangerous stage. Its rise also played a part, by increasing the risk that Baraka would fall ill in the first place. In luring millions of new people to the lake, the Nile perch boom made it easier for the bilharzia parasite to find human hosts in which to lay its eggs. It contributed, too, to the increase in snails, whose larva restarts the parasite's life-cycle. The snails' success was an unintended consequence of the introduction of the perch to Lake Victoria. For among the repercussions of the colonisers' decision to import the great predator was the extinction of most of the lake's cichlids.

Cichlids have an extraordinary ability to mutate in order to seize opportunities or evade threats. They can alter feeding strategies when a food source disappears, and change morphologically when stronger jaws, larger fins or differently shaped bodies would enhance their prospects of finding prey. To escape predators they can evolve to change colour, swim faster or deeper, or adapt to living in caves or under rocks. Such was their success that by the 1970s they dominated the lake, accounting for eighty per cent of its fish biomass.

But evolutionary prowess couldn't protect the cichlids against the onslaught that hit Lake Victoria in the ensuing decades. At their peak there had been as many cichlid species in the lake as there were freshwater fish species in the whole of Europe. But in the 1980s and 1990s more than two hundred species disappeared as their share of the fish biomass fell to just one per cent. In the late 1970s, a typical daily catch at a given point in Mwanza Gulf would contain at least nine thousand cichlids. At the same location in 1987, only three were caught in the whole year. A marine biologist from Boston University described what was happening as 'the greatest vertebrate mass extinction in recorded history.' Scientists who had once come to study the lake's biodiversity now came to observe its ruin.

The demise of the cichlids had three main causes. The most obvious was the Nile perch. Frans Witte, a Dutch scientist who until his death in 2013 had studied Lake Victoria's cichlids since the 1970s, found that extinction rates were much slower among those species that lived among rocks than among those that inhabited the open waters and were therefore more vulnerable to the perch's attacks. Species disappeared more slowly, too, in parts of the lake where perch were scarce. The introduction of the perch had not only presented the cichlids with a voracious new predator, moreover; the *sangara* competed with them for food, and its superior strength and its ability to consume its prey quickly put its much smaller, slow-eating rivals at a disadvantage.

Overfishing has also taken a toll, not just on Nile perch but on all the other fish in the lake, which are hoovered up as by-catch in the ever-more-efficient nets. Bait fishermen like Hasani have exacerbated the problem, while the growing demand for fishmeal to feed the livestock that are needed to sustain the burgeoning lacustrine population has swept up cichlids, *dagaa* and anything else the fishing fleets can lay their nets on.

But cichlid extinctions did not occur only in heavily fished parts of the lake. Nor were they limited to areas with large concentrations of Nile perch. That the fish also disappeared in untouched waters points to a third factor behind the loss of so many species. As the human population around the lake has swelled, it has polluted its waters. Factories – the fish processing factories as well as breweries, tanneries, paper mills and others attracted to the region by the scent of prosperity – have been allowed to dump their waste into the water with impunity. On the Tanzanian side alone, more than two million litres of sewage and industrial waste flow into the lake every day. Deforestation – to free up land for farms and fishing camps, build houses, fuel cooking fires and smoke the *sangara* – has loosened the soil, clearing the way for fertilisers, pesticides, animal feed and manure to be washed into the lake from the farms that abut its shores. So many nutrients oozing into the shallows are a boon to the algae that feed on them, and anyone flying over the lake will be struck by the vast blue-green algal clouds swirling below its surface. As it decays and sinks, this algae is broken down by microbes which suck oxygen from the water as they work – a process known as eutrophication. Without oxygen the cichlids can no longer breathe. Parts of the lake have become unfit for life.

The disappearance of so many cichlids has triggered vicious spirals that have hastened their downfall. A number of cichlid species fed on algae, and as these open-water swimmers were wiped out by the Nile perch the algal blooms grew larger, speeding the deoxygenation of the lake. Others fed on plant and animal matter that they found decomposing on the lake floor, thereby recycling the nutrients it contained back into the food chain. When these detritivores died out, rotting carcasses and plants began to silt up the depths – divers have found the lake bed to be strewn with dead and dying organisms – and as these were broken down by microbes, oxygen levels fell still further. The deeper waters became dead zones, and currents of oxygen-depleted water welling up from the bottom of the lake caused a growing number of mass fish die-offs.

The eutrophication of the lake has triggered a further vicious spiral by making it murkier. In the 1930s, a white disc held in the water could be seen to a depth of five metres below the surface. Today you can barely see such a disc if you hold it at arm's length. This muddying of the waters makes it more difficult for cichlids to spot nets. It also imperils future generations by weakening the gene pool. The female of many cichlid species chooses a mate based on appearance – the bolder and brighter a male's colouring, the better his chance of mating (it is thought that females perceive stronger colours as an indicator of good health, which will be passed down to their offspring). But in murky waters the female can no longer make out different hues, and is forced to mate with whatever comes along. If she can find a partner at all in the gloom, it is not always possible to choose the fittest, healthiest male. The offspring of such a mating – and, in time, the breed as a whole – will be less robust, and less likely to survive.

The proliferation of snails in the lake was another consequence of the cichlids' disappearance. Lake Victoria's cichlids exhibit a wide variety of diets and feeding strategies. As well as those that feed on algae or detritus, there are species that feed on insects, plants, prawns or crabs. A number feed on other fish, and the least discerning on animal or human faeces. To make sure of a meal, elaborate techniques are deployed. Some cichlids have extendable jaws to suck their prey from crevices in rocks. Some feed on the scales of other fish, which they tear off after attacking their prey from the side. Cannibalistic species, meanwhile, acquire their food by ramming into mouth-brooding mothers to shock them into disgorging their young.

Snails are a further popular ingredient of many cichlids' diet. The lake was once home to dozens of mollusc-eaters. Some used a second set of jaws to help crush the snails' shells; others would suck them out of their sanctuaries, or dislodge them by smashing the shells against rocks. In the past, mollusc-eating cichlids helped to control the population of snails in the lake and, as a consequence, to limit the spread of bilharzia. Many, however, are now extinct. The silvery-blue *Haplochromis fischeri* has not been seen since the early 1990s. Other species have either vanished or are critically endangered.

As their numbers have declined, the risk to humans of catching bilharzia has grown. Tanzanians' health has improved over the past few decades – between 1998 and 2020, average life expectancy increased by fifteen years. But while the incidence of most diseases decreased, that of bilharzia climbed. In the country as a whole, more than fifty per cent of people are infected at any one time. In communities around the lake, more than eighty per cent are infected. Hundreds die of the disease every year. For the unsuspecting Baraka and others like him, the disappearance of the snail-eaters has proved catastrophic.

Twenty-Two

Our house has many attractions for the children of the neighbourhood. It is a way station on the walk back from school, our front step a place to relax for a while before continuing homeward where domestic chores await. It is a meeting point, being equidistant from a number of their houses and offering a shady, cool place to catch up, exchange news, hatch plans and chat to Ebru and me. And it is a venue for games, the clearing below the mango tree a perfect spot for making mud sculptures, playing football or pig-in-the-middle, or running around pushing a wheel rim with a stick, and the tree itself ideal for climbing and, during the season, a source of delicious mangoes to suck on.

In some ways, too, the house is a source of wonder. The youngest children – Ali, Magesa, Lisa and Dolly, who are too young to attend Mwalimu's school – spend hours exploring its few amenities. They marvel at being able to press a switch that illuminates a distant light bulb, and recoil as if they have seen a snake when I tell them not to go near the plug sockets. They rest their cheeks on the cool floor tiles and turn the taps in the kitchen sink in the vain hope of producing water. The older children are more interested in our laptops and phones. They are spellbound when we let them listen to music through headphones. They huddle around when we show them photographs of our families – 'Look! They're white too!' – or of our former home in Europe or places we've visited elsewhere in Africa. Although neither they nor their parents have smartphones of their own, they immediately work out how to swipe through or enlarge photos.

The refrigerator in our living room is a source of particular fascination. It becomes so because of Riziki, a short-haired, round-faced ten-year-old who lives with her mother in a house by the lake. Riziki's name means "God's Blessing" and she is a sweet, warm-natured girl with a broad smile. Some islanders, though, regard her less as a blessing than a curse. One day while we are sitting talking to her on our step, Joshua informs us, in English, that Riziki is 'mentally handicapped' (until then I had attributed the slight slackness in her jaw and occasional slurring of her speech to physical causes). When she reaches adulthood, Joshua says, this will make it difficult for her to find a husband; more likely she will have to continue to rely on her mother for support. Even if someone can be found to marry her, he adds, the dowry her mother receives will be small, and being seen as cursed will render her more vulnerable to mistreatment by the groom and his family.

As a child, Riziki's life is not greatly affected by her disability. She attends school and is popular with the other children and especially with her inseparable friend Jenny; there is no indication that they, unlike their adult peers, think of her as any different to them. Nor does she lack creativity, and her schemes are as likely to be adopted by her peers as those of any other child.

When we had started buying water every day from Mama Neema or Centurio, we had worried that the discarded plastic bottles would be a pollutant. Our neighbours produce scarcely any waste. Their food comes directly from the fields or the lake and their second-hand clothes come without packaging from Europe and America. Anything that can be repaired is taken to a *fundi*, a job title that seems to cover anyone who can fix or make anything. Torn plastic buckets are sewn up with wires, flip-flops with glue or string. Shattered mobile phone screens are patched with sellotape or sticking plasters. Children wear their T-shirts until the holes are bigger than the fabric.

Since there are no garbage disposal facilities on the island, any rubbish is either abandoned or burned. Our culinary and sanitary habits mean we inevitably produce a small quantity of refuse, which we deposit in a shallow pit behind the house for Dickson to burn after he and the children have rummaged through it. Our water bottles, on the other hand, are recycled. During our stay on the island we would get through several hundred of these bottles. Not one would be wasted. A couple of dozen we used ourselves, at first for storing tap water and later, when the supply was cut off for good, the well-water we bought from an itinerant vendor. We gave a few bottles to Kitina for his banana beer and a few to our cycling milkman Ramek. Our neighbours took care of the rest, the children to use as flasks at school, their parents for storing grain, sugar, salt and water.

Riziki was the first to use them as an icebox. One rainy morning she came to our door bearing a full water bottle and asked me with a shy smile to put it in the fridge. An hour later she came back to retrieve it. She held it to her cheek like a cuddly toy, gulped down some of the cool liquid, then ran off, her large eyes almost popping out of her head with excitement, to tell her friends about her discovery.

Soon our fridge was full of bottles, our step strewn with children waiting for the miracle to come to pass. Riziki then asked me if we had a freezer. I am not sure how she knew about the latter, since it was unlikely that anyone she knew owned one, but when I told her that the lower half of our refrigerator was indeed a freezer, she asked for her bottle to be placed in there. Half an hour later I found her waiting for it on the step outside. I felt like the gypsy Melquíades as I explained that it would take a little longer for the water to turn into ice, but she said that she was happy to wait. Ice proved much more popular with the children than mere cold water, and the fad was only brought to an end when we noticed that several of them were developing coughs, which we feared might be aggravated by the ice.

Our daily walks into Nansio under the blazing early afternoon sun take us up the ochre-coloured road past a small open-air market known as Sungura. Sungura is Swahili for rabbit, which is the nickname given to a wiry old man who lives in the area who is famous for his reproductive prowess. These days Sungura clears drainage ditches for the local council, but he was once a man of influence, and after he purchased the island's first television set the market was named, informally at least, in his honour.

The area has a reputation for crime. As we walk towards it we are invariably heckled with shouts of "Mzungu". We buy bananas, onions and tomatoes from its thinly stocked stalls, and on occasion sit on a bench to drink *uji* served by a friendly mama. Penetrating the market's lanes, we find, silences the shouters, but it sparks instead more concerted conversations about us, which the *uji* seller politely pretends to ignore.

Nansio itself is remarkable only for its dereliction. Its two stretches of potholed paved road disintegrate into dust after a few hundred yards. Buckled tin roofs sag between the crumbling walls of what were once stores. On Wahindi Street – the street of the Indians – Art Deco buildings from the fifties and sixties are now piles of rubble, their Asian owners having long since moved back to the mainland or to India. More recent construction projects stand unfinished; the town has only a scattering of two-storey buildings, but several other would-be high-rises lie abandoned, the steel rods protruding from the tops of their ground-floor walls the only signs of the dashed ambitions of their owners.

One of the two-storey buildings belongs to La Bima Hotel. The hotel's accommodation area is of a single storey, but its bar boasts a new wooden construction on whose upper floor, reached by an uneven staircase, Ebru and I now and then take lunch. The building's precarious state means that we usually have the space to ourselves. Its distant view of the lake and the green hills that slide into it is a calming contrast to the occasional abrasiveness of the town below. We are served, eventually, with tilapia or Nile perch, accompanied – except on the rare days when the staff have remembered to switch on the refrigerator – by warm *Kilimanjaro* lager. Although we have come to cherish our neighbourhood, its surfeit of children means that it is seldom quiet in the afternoons, and our lunches out are a welcome respite.

The hotel wakes from its slumber only on evenings when there is a big Premier or Champions League football match on television. Most male islanders support one of the big English clubs, and for those who can afford a beer or a sachet or bottle of rum, the bar is a popular venue for watching important games (those with less spare cash can pay a few pennies to watch in a video hall). The picture is grainy, and frequent power cuts can make for a frustrating watch. Spectators, moreover, are at the mercy of the man who pays for the satellite TV subscription. This entrepreneur – the only person on Ukerewe with a legal connection – pays a monthly fee to the TV company and sublets lines to others. His clients, who as well as the aforementioned video halls include Mama Neema more than half a mile away in our district, are allowed for a small sum to string a wire to his receiver. The only problem for their customers is that they have no choice but to watch the channel of the entrepreneur's choosing. If he grows bored of a particular match he will change channel to watch another, or to watch a film or the news. This prompts loud groans among audiences across Nansio, but the entrepreneur, ensconced happily at home on his sofa, is oblivious to their frustration.

Although it is not a full-time brothel, La Bima's rooms, like those of all hotels in the lake region, are not used solely for rest. Towards the end of our stay we warn our cleaner Neema that we won't be around for much longer and advise her to start looking for another job. Her first port of call is Mabiba, but the pastor tells her there are no vacancies either at the church or as his housekeeper. When she tells him that she will have to look for a job in a guesthouse or a bar – there are few other employers on the island – he tells her it would be a sin to work in a place that serves alcohol. Neema has by now had her second child, a boy, and can't afford such scruples. When she asks Mabiba, who had insisted she have the child rather than abort it, what he suggests she should do instead, he tells her to stay at home and pray. 'God will help you,' he assures her.

Neema has no truck with this line of thinking, and she asks the manager of La Bima for a job as a waitress. Having worked for two foreigners turns out to be sufficient recommendation – the manager calls me for a reference – but the job turns out to be more challenging than she expected. Part of her role, it transpires, is to allow the bar's male customers to proposition her. Another is to allow them to grope her. Her colleagues, she tells me when she comes to visit one day, have sex with the customers for money after the bar has closed. Neema is appalled by this, but when she complained to the manager he told her that if she didn't like it she could leave. He pointed out, correctly, that there are plenty of other women to take her place.

With two children to feed by herself, Neema is cornered. She puts up with the groping and leering for a month, then has a lucky break when the manager offers her a new job as a receptionist in the hotel. This entails starting work at nine in the morning and finishing at eight in the evening, but Neema is delighted. Her fellow waitresses, too, are happy that she is not leaving, although they remain bemused, she tells me, by her reluctance to supplement her income by sleeping with the customers.

Many of the archipelago's bars host full-time sex workers as well as moonlighting waitresses. They sit in groups by the entrance and chat up men as they come in. A few of the women rent rooms in our neighbourhood. They dress differently to our other neighbours – they sport wigs or hair extensions and wear jeans under their wraparound skirts. Before they leave home in the evenings they put on make-up, which the likes of Lilian and Cristina never use, and they are more confident in their conversations with men. In the old days prostitutes made a good living on the island, and those who live near us still have a few appurtenances of wealth such as Western clothes or the radios they switch on when they return home late at night. Since the fishing boom fizzled out, however, many have gone elsewhere to seek their fortune. Nowadays men must turn to part-timers – women who dabble in sex work while spending the majority of their time farming or working in the markets. Some fishermen make use of female fish traders, who are forced by the scarcity of *sangara* to provide sexual favours in return for the right to sell a crew's catch.

It is not only the sex workers who are jumping ship. Two months before the end of our stay, our proselytising rickshaw driver Rama leaves for southern Tanzania with his wife and children. He can no longer make ends meet here, he explains. Ebru's taxi driver Nurdin follows soon after, his wife having grown tired of living in such a backwater and the income from his struggling business insufficient to compensate for being so cut off from the outside world. After many years on the archipelago, Centurio, too, is forced to leave. His new store has failed, he says. People on Kweru Mto had got used to him, and business there had been good until he fell ill. On Ukerewe, on the other hand, he is an outsider – an *Mzinza*, not an *Mkerewe* – and in a crumbling economy it has proved impossible to gain a foothold. He tells me he will return to his hometown by the lakeshore on the mainland and try to feed his children by farming instead. There he has access to a plot of family land that is larger than anything he can hope to acquire on Ukerewe. If the weather favours him, he and his wife, working hard together, might after a few years be able to produce a surplus, which will allow him to try his luck again in business.

Centurio knows that the weather is an unlikely ally. In

centuries past, Ukerewe had a benign climate, with reliable and plentiful rainfall. Annual precipitation in the early part of the twentieth century exceeded fifty inches, double that in parts of central Tanzania. Droughts were so rare that they were remembered for decades, and the chiefs who presided over them were either feared for their awesome power to fend off the rain or deposed for their incompetence.

Today, the average annual rainfall has declined by a fifth. Some years the island sees only a few inches. According to Hasani, the fishing crisis has been made worse by the lack of rain to flush food for the fish from the rivers into the lake. Even the ferry is affected by the changing climate – as the water level of Lake Victoria has fallen, the landing stage, which itself replaced a higher jetty by the old arrivals hall, has had to be extended ever farther into the lake.

In our second year on the island, the long rains fail. They are supposed to begin in early March, but by April barely a drop of rain has fallen. The few clouds that appear in the sky continue on their way, intact. Maize withers in the fields. Rice plants dry to husks before they can be harvested. Oranges, an important cash crop, shrivel in the trees. 'There will be hunger this year,' Centurio says, as listless as everyone else. The dust, blown into mouths and noses by the hot wind, makes the children sick.

One afternoon I ride out with Hasani and Lilian to their *shamba*. An unfenced half-acre plot a few miles east of our neighbourhood, the family briefly lived on it a few years back before moving closer to Nansio. Now they use it to cultivate beans, maize, cassava and sweet potatoes. Everything they grow they eat, after carting it home on their backs, their heads or on the seat of a rented bicycle. Farming here is generally a woman's responsibility, but Hasani helps Lilian out at planting and harvest time, or when the lake has been too rough for fishing.

While his wife bends over a patch of dry soil plucking out

weeds, Hasani shows me around the smallholding. It is not only this year, he tells me, that the weather has been unfavourable for farming. Even when they don't fail altogether, the rainy seasons are shorter than they used to be, and the downpours are often so hard that they wash away the topsoil and drown any crops that have survived the drought.

The *shamba*'s distance from their home is a drawback. Hasani shows me a stand of banana trees whose fruit has been freshly torn off. 'People who live nearby steal our crops,' he says. 'We are outsiders here so nobody does anything to stop it. The local people stick together.' His tone is resigned rather than angry, but for a family reliant on home-grown produce to keep its members strong enough to fend off disease, crop theft can be a death sentence.

Thieves in Tanzania play a dangerous game. The police are ineffective, but if they are apprehended by their fellow citizens they risk a lynching. I had heard of one recent case where a thief had been beaten to death by a mob, another where a tyre had been placed around the miscreant's neck, soaked in petrol and set alight. One morning we had been woken by a group of some thirty men and women running past the house, laughing and shouting as they chased a chicken thief. The man reached the police station before the crowd could get its hands on him, his sprinting speed possibly saving his life. 'We are poor,' Hasani had said when I asked him if he approved of such vigilante justice. 'We work hard for money and spend our whole lives trying to get it. Thieves come along and take it without working for it. They deserve to be punished.'

As the drought persists, prices in the markets rise. A kilo of rice doubles in price in a fortnight. The price of maize climbs above what many can afford. Sweet potatoes, the thirstiest of the staples, are nowhere to be seen. Matters become so serious that even the local council grows concerned. Food handouts are planned, and officials traipse around the villages trying to establish who is poor enough to need one. In our district everybody qualifies, and each household will receive a bucketful of maize. One bucketful ever, that is, not one a week or one a month. Tanzania's government is not interested in Ukerewe, whose member of parliament belongs to the opposition party, and in a place where there is no money to pay for electricity to operate the island's water pump, a sustained food distribution campaign would be impossible.

Twenty-Three

Joshua talks often about joining the exodus. Having spent much of his youth in Dar es Salaam, he regards living on the island as a backward step, a humiliation. The dearth of work opportunities means he cannot earn enough to set up as an adult – to take a wife, build a house, or have children other than the four or five he has spawned during brief flings but no longer has anything to do with. Nor is he of much use to his mother, who whenever she needs food or medicine asks his despised older brother instead for help. As his brother continues to thrive while he continues to flounder, the idea of moving away becomes ever more attractive.

First, though, he must amass some capital. His house painting business is not working out. Few islanders these days can afford to build or decorate houses, and those who do have the means to begin such projects often run out of cash before they can pay their contractors. The African informal sector is idealised by many economists, who regard it as an enterprising, resilient system that compensates for the continent's lack of formal sector jobs. But working in the black market is fraught with risk. Joshua frequently starts jobs that are abandoned after he has bought the paint (to pay for which he has usually had to borrow from friends). Sometimes he finishes jobs for which he is never paid. One recent client fled the island as soon the work was done – since he rents the house out to a tenant, he need never return. Another told Joshua to prepare the paint and that he would give him an advance for the work later that day. When no advance was forthcoming, Joshua put the job on hold – now that he had completed the skilled work of mixing the paint, he predicted, the client would find someone cheaper to do the painting itself.

Because he works without formal contracts, Joshua has no

recourse. But if he registers as a formal business, with all the costs that entails in fees, bribes, time and taxes, other painters will undercut him. After his latest setback, for the first time in the year we had known him Joshua had been reduced to coming to our door to ask for food (on another occasion when he had had to kill his last hen because he and his mother had nothing to eat, he had come round to ask if we needed any of the meat). 'I'm so hungry,' he said. 'I've tried everywhere for food – I'm sorry I have to come to you.'

In his search for capital, he tries a number of avenues. We persuade a friend who runs the bar at the hotel by the lake to interview him for a barman position, but the smell of alcohol on his breath betrays him and he is rejected. His bus accident has left him too weak to farm, so he tries his hand instead in the used-clothing trade. I lend him a few dollars to help him buy his first sack of European cast-offs from Mwanza, and he takes it to a field on the edge of our neighbourhood where there is a Sunday morning clothes market. The market is crammed with competitors, several of whom have ear-splitting loudhailers to assist them, but Joshua has a winning way with customers and for a few weeks he does well. He specialises in shirts and T-shirts, and when he has sold one sackful he goes to Mwanza to buy another. Each shirt costs less than a dollar, but his profits give him a little breathing space – he can afford to buy a few fish to garnish his *ugali*, and he buys his mother a new chicken.

Around here, however, success does not go unnoticed. One Sunday night, three men break into the room in which Joshua sleeps. He tries to fight them off, but in the scuffle his forearm is cut by a machete and one of his front teeth knocked out by an iron bar. The thieves make off with all the cash he has taken that day. He is left without a penny to his name.

He tells me all this a few days later, on our return from a visit to the mainland. I ask him if he knows the men. 'It was too dark to see their faces,' he replies. 'But people here are witches. They can see these things. They know who it was, but I can't tell you.'

It takes me a couple of days to prise the secret from him. The witches, it turns out, are pointing the finger at Hasani – hence Joshua's reluctance to tell me. The reason for the rumours is envy.

For Hasani, too, is resented. The fisherman is worried that if one day he is crippled by bilharzia and no longer brings in an income, Lilian will be unable to afford the five-dollar monthly rent they pay for the room the family lives in. He therefore plans to build them a house of their own. He has acquired a small plot of land to the rear of Sungura market, and has begun to amass the fifteen hundred bricks that will be required to build a two-room house with an outside toilet. To make the bricks, he, Lilian and their eldest children take buckets to the lake and fill them with sand from the lake floor. They carry the buckets on their heads to a brickmaker, who mixes the sand with a little cement and moulds it into shape. Then they take the bricks back to the yard behind their house, and leave them in rows to dry.

Hasani estimates that the whole project – making the bricks, hiring a builder, and buying rocks for the foundations, tin for the roof and wood for the door and unglazed windows – will cost just over five hundred dollars. Sitting with him on his log one night watching fireflies flitting in the warm darkness, I ask how long it will take to save the money. He takes a drag on his spindly joint. 'About five years,' he replies, 'God willing.'

That the process will be slow and painstaking, however, does not shield the family from the jealousy of their neighbours. Building a house – even one with no running water or electricity in a district with a reputation for criminality – is a mark of success. In such a poor community, it's seen by some as an attempt to rise above one's proper station, a rejection of the solidarity encouraged by the father of the nation Nyerere, whereby all are supposed to be poor together. Rumours have been swirling that Hasani has been using illicit means to raise the funds to have the bricks made. The burglary confirms the backbiters' suspicions.

On the night of the crime, Hasani was fishing on the lake. He has often helped Joshua out, lending him the tarpaulins on which he lays out his clothes at the market and giving him money for malaria medication or food when he needs it (most islanders catch malaria once or twice a year). Joshua knows all this, but his respect for the witches is such that he is nevertheless thinking about reporting his friend to the police. I try hard to deter him. Hasani is unlikely to have had anything to do with the incident, and the police – even with no evidence but witches' chatter – will extract a debilitating bribe to let him go free. Joshua is too intelligent to allow scurrilous gossip completely to overrule logic, but it takes days of cajoling to divert him from his course.

His business briefly recovers from this blow, but when a few weeks later a trader in Mwanza sells him a sack full of damaged clothes – buyers are not allowed to check the sealed bags' contents – he decides to depart for Dar es Salaam even without the capital he hoped to have accumulated. 'There is nothing for me here,' he tells us. In the city he will lodge with his late brother's widow, who lives in one of its outlying slums, and peddle whatever he can lay his hands on. We help him with the bus fare and see him on his way to the ferry. With him he takes a small holdall that contains everything he owns in the world.

Hasani, who appears to know nothing of how close he came to being arrested for a crime he didn't commit, doesn't have the option of leaving. The only craft he knows is fishing, and although his method is illegal he has no choice but to continue until he is caught. In recent years it has become riskier to ply his trade. A new president has come to power in Tanzania, a stubborn, autocratic figure who brooks no dissent. He is fond of simple solutions to complex problems, blunt measures he can trumpet for their boldness in a media he is cowing into submission. His solution to the Lake Victoria crisis is to crack down on illegal fishing, and in particular on *kokoro* fishermen like Hasani. Patrols have been stepped up, punishments stiffened. *Kokoro* fishermen are an easy target – the poorest of those working on the lake, they have no power to demand compensation in return for giving up their livelihoods, and no means of bribing those who enforce the law. Many of Hasani's peers have had their nets confiscated and burned. Some, unable to pay fines, have been locked up in the island's Dickensian prison. None has been offered an alternative means of making a living. Cash or credit might encourage them to purchase legal nets and to fish from boats rather than beaches; retraining programmes might help them learn a new trade. But with the government preferring sticks to carrots and valuing quick fixes and headlines over understanding and consensus, no such assistance is forthcoming.

Hasani treats his plight with calm resignation. He moves his net-mending activities behind a neighbour's building, out of sight of the road, and makes sure he and his crew are back from the lake before rather than after dawn each morning. When the new government insists that patrol boats go out at night despite the dangers, many of those he fishes with grow too fearful to work. Often he cannot find three other crewmembers to fill his boat. This too he accepts with equanimity. He cuts back on the number of days he fishes and puts his trust in fate. 'God is great,' he replies simply, when I ask if he is worried.

Banning *kokoro* fishing is not the only possible solution to the collapse of the fishing industry. It may not even be the best solution. The effectiveness of a ban is far from guaranteed – the lake is vast, the fishermen know it better than the authorities, and in the absence of alternative income sources they have no choice but to continue to try to break the law. And although it will reduce the culling of young and breeding Nile perch, the ban will not put an end to overfishing in deeper waters. As Hasani points out, the number of fish is declining even though there are hundreds of miles of shoreline with no beach seiners.

The local council has attempted to do its part to stem the decline of the fish by planting bushes in the shallows. Nile perch breed in the shelter of such bushes, and their young loiter there until they are strong enough to withstand the rigours of the open lake. The problem with this plan is that bushes are made of wood, and in a community where only a minority of households can afford to buy gas or kerosene to cook their food, wood is a valuable commodity. On an island denuded of trees, and with free wood today considered more important than well-grown fish tomorrow, the bushes are soon razed to the ground.

More serious measures would require either greater investment or a willingness to step on the toes of powerful interests. Enforcing bans on the industrial pollution of the lake or the selling of undersized fish by fish factories would mean taking on wealthy businessmen who have links to the political classes. Building sewage treatment facilities in the lakeshore towns and putting toilets near the beaches would incur large costs for no glory (photographs of a politician standing by a long-drop toilet being less impressive than a new stadium or bridge). Reducing the number of fishermen – both illegal and legal – by providing them with alternative income sources such as jobs or the capital to set up businesses would also require investment, as well as ingenuity in a country with little formal sector employment. It is cheaper – at least in the short-term during which a president might expect to be in power – to burn nets and levy fines.

A potential solution to Hasani's predicament comes from an unlikely quarter. One afternoon Ebru and I head to the overgrown garden of the lakeside hotel for a ginger beer. Sitting in the shade of a slowly collapsing gazebo, we watch kites wheeling over the calm lake and a jet-black open-billed stork prancing on the narrow strand of beach. A yellow and blue lizard does press-ups on the low, crumbling boundary wall as we studiously divert our eyes from the naked bathers in the shallows.

After a while we are joined at our table by Mabiba, who is still living in the hotel. For several months he has behaved coolly towards us, possibly because he believes we have led Neema astray, but today he is friendlier. Life, he says, is going well. He has embarked on a new business venture, the latest step in the construction of his Christian business empire. The project is a partnership with a white man. It will not only transform the island, he declares; it will save the lake in the process.

We would meet the white man, who is also staying at the hotel, for an evening beer a few days later. A short, grizzled-looking Italian in his forties named Matteo, he is an aquaculture expert, and he is here to persuade and help local fishermen to diversify into fish farms. His motivations are more philanthropic than Mabiba's – he has spent the last few years working for an NGO in the Ivory Coast – but the pastor has convinced him to treat his work as a means of both doing good and making money, and the two of them plan to act as middlemen between the producers and buyers of the farms' harvest.

Further north in Africa, aquaculture has a long pedigree: four thousand years ago a tomb-painter in the Nile Valley in Egypt depicted a man sitting by an artificial tank fishing with a rod for tilapia. But at the great river's source, the concept is a new one. Ukerewe has less than half a dozen fish farms. There are two near the ferry dock – tennis court-sized pits of black water which are a haven for lake flies and mosquitoes – and another near Dina Charles's village to the west. If the World Bank has its way, it will soon have many more. In better times, the bank helped fund the establishment of the fish processing factories that have laid waste to the lake. Now it sees the farms as a solution to the decline in fish stocks, and particularly as a means of curbing illegal fishing. It has made grants available to extend the practice around the lake, and Matteo and Mabiba are keen to piggyback on its latest big idea.

An expansion of fish farms has the potential to provide a more reliable income for those who manage them and relieve the pressure on Lake Victoria, but aquaculture is not uncontroversial. In some ways it might exacerbate existing problems. Industrial-scale production of tilapia – Matteo and the World Bank's chosen species – will push down the price of fish, and those crews still out on the lake will have to exploit it ever more intensively to maintain their income levels. Since farmed fish are kept in high concentrations in a confined space, moreover, they are vulnerable to the rapid spread of disease and parasites. If farmers cannot prevent these blights, there is a danger that they will infect the lake's wild fish. If fungicides and pesticides are used to ward them off, these too may leak into the open water. The ponds dug so far in Ukerewe are all within a few yards of the lakeshore. It would take only a slight rise in the water level to flush chemicals and uneaten fish food into a lake already suffocating under an excess of nutrients.

Mabiba is unaware of these risks, and Matteo believes that if the farms are well looked after their side effects can be minimised. The two men spend their days on the back of motorbike taxis, touring the island's fishing camps to promote the scheme to the fishermen and staking out lakeside villages to find suitable spots for ponds. When I tell Hasani about Matteo's work, he asks if he can meet him. He comes with me one day to the hotel garden, but after the Italian has explained his plans I can see that his enthusiasm has waned.

I ask him later what has put him off the idea. He says that to run a fish farm as a co-operative, which the donors are insisting on in order to occupy greater numbers of fishermen, he would need to join up with a team of other fishers. A few of these men would have to be tasked with guarding the ponds at night, but he doesn't know anybody he could trust with this role. I think back to what Bebe had told us about witch doctors sowing distrust in communities, and to the argument at the dock in Mwanza on the day of our arrival. 'They would either steal the fish themselves,' Hasani says, 'or let thieves steal them and take a commission.'

In the past, labour practices on the island were governed by a spirit of cooperation. Villagers helped each other with weeding, planting and harvesting. Fishermen kept an eye out for one another to ensure that everyone returned safely. That fellow clan members could be trusted was a given and those who dared to breach this trust were ostracised.

A collaborative approach was also adopted to managing the lake's resources. The clans looked upon the fish as a gift from God – how else but through divine intervention could the creatures have reached a body of water hundreds of miles inland? All had the right to partake of this gift, but none could claim ownership. The techniques that could be used, the parts of the lake that could be fished, and the times of year during which fishing was permitted were agreed between the elders and any other interested adults. Nobody was denied access to the lake, and those who were unable to fish had as much right to a share of its munificence as those who worked the shallows. When a fish was caught it belonged not to the catcher but to his community, and fishermen would present their catch to the chief or the clan elders to be shared among their fellows.

With colonialism, and continuing after independence, all this changed. Lake Victoria became state rather than communal property and the lakeshore governments took over its management. Once a provider of sustenance and a guarantor of food security, it was now treated as a source of income and a contributor to the public purse. For the people of Ukerewe, this meant that their access to the lake was no longer free, their right to fish no longer uncontested. As fishing became industrialised – and particularly as Nile perch became harder for artisanal fishermen to catch – many had no choice but to work for others if they wished to continue to live off the lake. They took up employment with the processing factories, with agents connected to the factories, or with businessmen with high-level political connections who had taken over beaches or islands.

In their minds, however, nothing had changed. The lake and its contents were still a gift from God, and still belonged to no one. In a survey of fishermen at a beach near Mwanza at the peak of the boom, nearly all respondents said that anybody who wanted to fish on the lake should be allowed to. The waters, they said, belonged to either everybody or nobody. Only one in three said they belonged to the state. Government control of the lake was seen as useful if it helped maintain the number of fish, but if it contravened the communal ethos it would be rejected.

The Beach Management Units, which were set up around the lake to mitigate the fishing collapse, paid no heed to these sentiments. They were imposed by government Fisheries Departments and peddled regulations drawn up by bureaucrats in distant capitals. Those affected by the regulations, and by the new punishments that came with them, played no part in their development. The old ways – long deliberations between fishermen and community elders, the patient forging of agreement – were deemed no longer fit for purpose. The fishermen now had to do what the Fisheries Departments and their minions wanted. That Hasani and many others ignored the new strictures was inevitable – these emissaries of a far-off authority had done nothing to earn their respect, and nothing to deserve their obedience.

The competition for the declining fish stocks has hastened the disintegration of the old values. The tragedy of the commons has ended in a desperate free-for-all, a mass looting of the lake.

The co-operative model espoused by Matteo is doomed by the pervasive mistrust. Within months both he and Mabiba would leave the island, their project in tatters. Hasani, staying on, continued to fish from the beaches.

Twenty-Four

One morning a few weeks before we are to leave, Neema surprises us by visiting our house. Since she has started working at La Bima we have seen less of her, her working hours too long for much socialising. She has on a maroon dress made of a material so shiny it looks as if she is on her way to a wedding, and is accompanied by a young man with a camera. The man is a professional photographer, she says, and she has hired him to take her picture with us, her former employers, so that she can remember us once we are gone.

The most difficult aspect of our imminent departure is having to wrench ourselves away from the children. Twenty of them spend much of their free time either sitting on our step or playing on the patch of ground under the mango tree in front of our house. We have got to know them well, from the early days when three of the bravest came over to introduce themselves, to more recent afternoons when they have sat playing cards or looking at books in our living room. We have suffered through fraught evenings with them, tending to their illnesses and worrying that their fever was climbing beyond what their undernourished bodies could bear. We have depended on them – for moral support in the early days when their parents were still wary of us, and for companionship and entertainment when we have sat and chatted with them, helped them with their homework or simply watched them at play. So close have we grown to them that one of them, Pascali, dubs himself and his friends "Brother Mark and Sister Ebru's Kids".

In our last week I walk into town with Pascali and Saidi to buy them a football as a goodbye present. We have bought them perhaps a dozen balls during our time on the island – small ones for the little kids, full-sized ones for their elders. Few have remained intact for more than a day or two, torn by rocks or stray shards of glass, but by having them patched up by an adult they have wrung a few weeks of life out of each one before returning to their string and plastic bag concoctions when there was nothing left to sew together.

This time they have asked for a leather ball, which they believe will be robust to whatever the island's ragged ground can throw at it. In the market I pay three times as much for it as for the rubber balls we have previously bought (two days later they would come round to show me a huge gash in the costly fabric), and Saidi then asks if I can buy them a pair of goalkeeper's gloves. Shocked by the price of the ball, he says they will haggle for these themselves. 'If they see a white man like you,' he explains, 'they will double the price.'

I wait for them at the juice bar on Nansio's main street, opposite the market. Here you can sit on pliant plastic chairs, shielded from the sun by a tall tree and from the road by a drainage ditch crossed via a wooden plank, and drink fresh, unadulterated juice while watching the comings and goings of the town. I order a glass of avocado juice from the waitress, a shy young woman in a white apron and chef's cap. To my right as I sit facing the street is a ladies' clothes store from whose tin roof hang colourful dresses that balloon below the hip (large bottoms being as prized in these parts as pale skin). In front of the store by the street, a rickety wooden stand bears a tray of the green oranges for which Ukerewe is famed. A little further along, a cobbler squats on a wooden chair that barely rises above ground-level, surrounded by his tools and a clutch of onlookers as he sews up torn flip-flops with string. Beside him waits a phalanx of motorbike taxi drivers, young men leaning forward onto their handlebars as they discuss passers-by, English or Tanzanian football teams, and the girls they hope to bed.

To my left, outside a store that appears at any one time to stock no more than half a dozen second-hand spare parts for motorbikes, two young men sit on crates playing carom, a legacy of the long-forgotten Indian presence on the island. Men wandering by stop to watch and comment as the players flick counters across the vast board balanced between them on their knees. Beyond them is a small shack made of corrugated iron which sells and rents out newspapers. A posse of men and boys huddles before its single shelf reading the headlines. For a while the teenager who ran the shack stocked a weekly English-language paper, *The East African*, but I was deprived of this luxury when the government banned it over a cartoon that had offended the president by implying that he was corrupt.

Most of the time the street is quiet and drowsy in the tropical heat. Activity is limited to the occasional passage of water sellers pushing trolleys laden with jerrycans, or of children hawking peanuts or bananas carried in trays on their heads. In the cavernous liquor store opposite the juice bar, men recline on boxes drinking beer or rum while they watch football replays on a grainy television set. Those with more earnest purposes flit in and out of an internet café next door, printing CVs or searching for online agents who promise to secure them visas to Europe. On street corners teenagers under umbrellas sell mobile phone top-up vouchers. Stout market women with buckets on their heads rewrap their *kanga* cloths around their waists as they stride heavily past.

Only at midday or in the early evening, when the ferry arrives from Mwanza, does the street come to life. The boat spews foot passengers from the dock carrying heavy suitcases or baskets. Many make for the shared taxi stand a mile up the road. Here they pack into battered estate cars to be driven to villages in the interior of the island, or to jetties on the northern shore where they will board motorised canoes to distant islets. Those who can afford it catch motorbike taxis to the stand, or pay porters a few cents to cart their luggage in trolleys. In the middle of the town, trucks disgorged from the ferry stop by the side of the street. Young day labourers swarm aboard them to unload the cargo, like leaping lions assailing an exhausted elephant. The faces of the new arrivals are happy and smiling, relieved to have safely negotiated the ferry crossing and warmed by the prospect of home.

Ferries setting out on the return journey to Mwanza are less orderly. The shared taxis from the interior plan their journeys to coincide with the ferries' scheduled departures. Their drivers aim to deposit their passengers at the taxi stand in good time for them to flag down a motorbike or walk the last mile to the jetty. This being rural Tanzania, however, where few possess functioning watches and people's sense of time is anyway unsuited to strict itineraries, many taxis arrive late. This is not always a problem – the ferry itself seldom departs punctually and delays of three or four hours are common. But taxi drivers and their passengers can never be sure what the ferry will do. Now and then it leaves at the designated hour. Depending on his mood, the captain doesn't always take pity on stragglers. Missing the afternoon ferry means being marooned on the island until at least the next morning, and the additional transport and accommodation costs can be crippling. Taxis that are running late therefore ignore the rule that obliges them to end their journey at the stand north of town, and instead make as quickly as possible for the jetty. Their horns blaring, they hurtle down the main street of Nansio, scattering goats, chickens, cyclists and pedestrians in their single-minded pursuit of their objective. Even motorbike taxis, themselves in a hurry to ensure their passengers make it to the ferry, must make way – size matters on Ukerewe's roads, and those on four wheels pay no attention to those on a mere two.

When the ferry finally leaves, the quiet returns. Foot passengers who have missed the boat make their disconsolate way homewards. The motorbike riders head back to their stations around town. And the now-empty shared taxis cruise languidly back towards the taxi stand as if nothing has happened.

After some time Saidi and Pascali turn up with their gloves, which they have acquired for about fifty cents. Hasani has tried to teach his children not to ask for things. On one occasion when I was complaining about strangers continually asking me for money, he told me that people will give if they want to give, not when they are asked. But with his father elsewhere, Saidi had been unable to resist, and as he takes the gloves from their packet to try them on his face beams with excitement.

Pascali chooses pineapple juice, Saidi avocado. We sit drinking through straws and watching cyclists weave by, both boys struggling to suppress smiles at the thrill of sitting here, drinking juice, with their foreign grown-up friend. 'How much does one glass cost?' Pascali asks. It is his first visit to the juice bar. I tell him the price. 'It's delicious,' he says. 'In future when I get any money I'll come here and have a juice.'

From his parents Pascali is unlikely to get any money. His father spends most of the little he earns from selling fish on drink, and his mother has moved to one of the smaller islands where she has married another man. Now and then Pascali makes a few shillings by selling bits of scrap metal he finds lying about, but it is him and his siblings Jenny and Peter for whom we are most fearful as our time on the island draws to a close. While none of the other children of the neighbourhood is well-off, each of them has at least one parent who works hard and either produces food by farming or brings in money from a small business. Pascali's father Juma is a hard worker himself – he leaves home for the beaches at dawn and returns well after dusk – but his alcohol craving and the decline of the fishing industry mean that his children seldom have enough to eat, and they are constantly beset by the stomach pangs associated with excessive hunger and the diseases that take advantage of their weakness.

It is difficult, however, to leave them with something that will be of use. In their single-room, sparsely furnished house there is nowhere to hide anything, and cash will be discovered by Juma and spent on sugarcane rum. Food will help in the short-term, and we buy them sacks of beans and rice in the market. Peter suggests a duck, but Pascali says ducks would be too easy for his father to sell. Finally Joshua, who has joined us in taking an interest in the three children's future, recommends a goat, and although to us a goat sounds no more fixed an asset than a duck, the children agree that this is the best way we can help them.

The goats of Ukerewe play an important role as insurance. Feeding them costs nothing, as they eat anything they find, and since they make no demands on their owner's finances they can be kept for many years. Only when disaster strikes a household are the animals sold. A funeral, a health setback, a fine for some real or invented infringement of the law, perhaps a large dowry payment – having a goat to sell can be a vital recourse in times of emergency.

Pascali asks for a nanny goat, which he can breed from if he can find a neighbour to lend him a male. I go with Joshua to find a goat seller he knows in a village a few miles inland. We walk for a couple of hours through a thinned-out forest, and when we reach the village – a few scattered mud houses in a clearing – Joshua makes enquiries and we sit on tree stumps to wait.

While we are sitting, shaded by tall trees, a puppy playing nearby reminds me that for the past couple of weeks the nocturnal howling and yelping of the street dogs around our house has unaccountably ratcheted up. It has been keeping us awake for at least an hour each night rather than the usual ten minutes in the early hours. I ask Joshua if he knows why the dogs have suddenly grown so vociferous. He is not sure, but he does know the reason for their nightly choruses. 'Dogs can see witches,' he says, slicing with a rusty knife a mango one of the village children has given him. 'They start to bark when the witches come out to do their work at two o'clock at night. Dogs and witches are enemies. They only stop barking after the witches have washed in the lake after finishing their work and gone home.'

I ask him how he knows all this, given that humans can't see witches. 'Some people have a gift,' he replies. 'They can see them. You could see them too if you took the right medicine.' He slips a slice of mango into his mouth. 'Do you ever hear the dogs barking in the daytime?' he asks me, munching. I have to admit that I don't.

After an hour the goat man arrives. He tells us he doesn't have any animals to sell at the moment. We walk back home, asking in several villages on the way if anybody wants to sell us a goat. When we are about a hundred yards from our house – having walked for miles in vain – we come upon a compound that is teeming with young goats. 'Hodi,' Joshua calls – the traditional greeting of arrival to see if anybody is around. 'Karibu,' someone shouts in welcome from inside one of the mud-brick houses. An elderly man in a loincloth and white vest emerges. He instructs us to take seats in the yard while his surprised wife brings us cups of steaming *uji*. At first he is reluctant to sell, but Joshua is a persuasive negotiator and after some discussion the man agrees to part with a nanny goat. Joshua insists that since the animal is not for me but for some impoverished local children, the man shouldn't increase the price simply because I am white. After a few more minutes of friendly haggling a sum is agreed with which he is satisfied. He hoists the chosen specimen onto his shoulders for the short walk home.

Pascali, Jenny and Peter welcome the addition to their household with overwhelmed smiles. Jenny runs off to grab some leaves for it from a bush. I ask Pascali where they will keep it. 'Inside the house,' he replies. The goat will share their room, safe from the grasp of thieves. In a few months, Pascali adds excitedly, it will be mature enough to breed from; his dream of a menagerie of goats snoring beside his thin, foam mattress will thereby be fulfilled.

Twenty-Five

On our last morning on the island I go over to chat to Hasani in his yard. He is sitting smoking a joint, and smiles as I approach. To one side Tatu is bathing the chubby Magesa in a washing-up tub. His body and head lathered in soap bubbles, Magesa, who hates being wet, is screaming at the top of his voice. Beside the tub stands Ali, awaiting his turn and giggling at his brother's antics. In the shade of the adjoining house, Cristina sits suckling her new baby girl, Veisa. She now has five children to bring up, most of the time by herself while her husband is away fishing. The oldest of them, Danny, aged nine, is over on our step, reading aloud an English book Ebru has given him (the children are on holiday from school). Beside him his younger sister Lisa, her hair newly braided, pulls the sides of her mouth to make a face.

Lilian brings out a chair for me to sit on and retreats inside. Hasani tells me he hasn't slept yet. His night on the lake brought in a total of about three dollars, to be shared between him and his crew. He will sleep after we leave on the afternoon ferry, he says – he must be around to see us off. After some time Lilian comes out again. 'Karibu chakula,' she says quietly – welcome for food. I tell her that we're planning to eat in town on our way to the ferry, so there's no need to give us such a send-off, but she insists I call Ebru and that we join them for lunch.

In their house we sit on a small sofa with beige cushions and wooden armrests. Hasani and Lilian sit on a similar sofa on the other side of a low table. The room, with its unglazed windows and bare concrete floor, is cool and dark. It is split in two by an orange sheet that hangs from the ceiling, separating the living area from the two beds on which they and the six children for whom they are currently responsible sleep. In the corner near the doorway a chicken pecks on the floor. Ali and Magesa come in after their bath to join us, kneeling at opposite ends of the table as they wait for their share of the food.

Called by Hasani, Joshua comes round and squeezes in beside us. Lilian tilts a jug over a plastic bowl and pours water on our hands. On the table she has set a large tin tray heaped with rice – an expensive concession to our mystifying aversion to *ugali* – and a smaller pot containing chunks of Nile perch in a thin broth. They must have bought the fish from a passing fishmonger – Hasani had told me he caught only a few *furu* that night. Their generosity increases our melancholy, and Ebru and I are subdued as we push a few morsels into our mouths with our fingers.

Lilian is surprised by how little we eat. She and Hasani urge us to take more, and laugh when we protest that they have six children to feed. Joshua tells us in English that we are making them happy by eating their food, and that providing hospitality to guests is their duty as well as a way of expressing their gratitude for the time we have spent with them and their children. That they have been a source of immense joy to us is immaterial. 'You must eat,' he says. Lilian smiles and nods, understanding the gist if not the words.

When we hear the arriving ferry's horn, we gather our bags outside our house, lock the gate and do the rounds of the neighbourhood to say goodbye. Mwalimu, whose school operates even during the holidays, breaks off from a lesson under his mango tree to wish us well. When he thanks us for spending time among them, Ebru's eyes fill with tears. Joshua's aging mother leans on the hoe with which she has been breaking the ground outside her house and says, 'Karibu tena' – welcome again. Public displays of affection are unusual around here, and Cristina shakes my hand with a curtsey before giving Ebru an awkward hug. Lilian does the same, although less awkwardly and without the curtsey. We hug Magesa, Dolly and Lisa, and shake hands with their older siblings and friends – Saidi, Tatu,

Rama, Devidi, Danny, Pascali, Peter, Jenny, Mazigo, Katondo, Mase and Zebe. Ali, who had as usual run over to our gate to greet us first thing in the morning, clutching the top of his trousers to stop them falling down, stands off to one side, unusually reticent. He is accustomed to us leaving for short periods, but seeing the crowd gathering in front of our house has realised that this time is more permanent. I pick him up and ask if he is all right. He nods his head, but remains quiet. There is a look of something approaching shock on his little round face.

Lilian, Hasani and Joshua accompany us along the dirt road for the first few yards of our journey. They wish us a safe trip, before returning to their lives. The older children escort us as far as Sungura market. When they turn back, too, smiling and waving, Ebru and I are left alone. In silence we continue towards Nansio under the burning midday sun, to answer the ferry's call.

Epilogue

The disappearance of so many Nile perch from the lake has eased the predatory pressure on other fish. In the last few years the decline of fish stocks has decelerated, and to the surprise of scientists, cichlid species that were long thought extinct have begun to reappear in nets.

To survive the depredations of the *sangara* and the eutrophication of the waters, cichlids have had to adapt. Some evolved stronger fins that enabled them to dodge the perch's lunge. Others changed their diet, rooting for food in areas the perch couldn't reach, or hybridised with other cichlids, collapsing two species into one. The orange-tailed *Haplochromis pyrrhocephalus* responded to the increased murkiness by switching its diet from zooplankton, which are small and translucent, to more visible prey such as shrimps and snails. This required it to hunt on the lake bed instead of at the surface, an oxygen-scarce environment where it would need stronger respiratory apparatus. To overcome this difficulty, its gill size expanded by two-thirds in just twenty years. Its mouth grew bigger, too, to accommodate the larger prey, while its eyes, no longer so important, shrank to compensate. In the late 1980s this finger-sized fish was considered extinct, but so rapid has been its resurrection that today it is not considered endangered.

Just as the lake has shown faint signs that it might one day recover, academics have begun to question the inevitability of the tragedy of the commons which helped cause the cichlids' demise. In 2009 Elinor Ostrom, a professor at Indiana University in the United States, became the first woman to win the Nobel Prize in Economics. Her research demonstrated that there have been a number of exceptions to the rule that common property is doomed to destruction. Over the centuries, she and her colleagues found, communities around the world have voluntarily organised themselves to manage fisheries and forests sustainably, without government involvement. Their members have shared the sacrifices needed to preserve a common resource, and shared in the resulting long-term rewards.

At the heart of these communities' success has been a collective ethos, whereby users of the resource help decide who can use it, when and how it can be used, and how transgressors should be punished. If governments ignore local communities' needs and opinions, Ostrom showed, they will be compelled to invest in costly and often-ineffective patrols – like those deployed in Lake Victoria – to enforce conservation measures. 'On the other hand,' she wrote, 'when the users themselves have a role in making local rules, or at least consider the rules to be legitimate, they are frequently willing to engage themselves in monitoring and sanctioning of uses considered illegal.'

For Ali, Lisa, Magesa and their friends, the future is likely to depend on both the resilience of the lake and a willingness to heed the lessons of the past. The approach Elinor Ostrom favoured has much in common with how the people of Ukerewe managed their fishery before the colonisers arrived. For the ancestors of today's islanders, its adoption would be not a revolution but a return to the norm.

Acknowledgements

My most obvious debt is to our neighbours and friends in Ukerewe, some of whose names have been changed here to protect their privacy, who as well as steadfast companionship and support, patiently gave me their time and shared their knowledge as I tried to get my head around their world.

I thank Maya Evans and Lewis Broadway for assistance with the cover design, Robin Davies, Barry Campbell, Gemma Willis, David Steven, Lisa Foreman and my parents for extremely helpful and detailed comments and advice, Nathan Thornburgh of Roads & Kingdoms for encouraging me to write about island life, and of course my wife Ebru for getting the job in Ukerewe in the first place and sticking with it through the difficult times.

The book is dedicated to the children.

EARTH BOOKS

ENVIRONMENT

Earth Books are practical, scientific and philosophical publications about our relationship with the environment. Earth Books explore sustainable ways of living; including green parenting, gardening, cooking and natural building. They also look at ecology, conservation and aspects of environmental science, including green energy. An understanding of the interdependence of all living things is central to Earth Books, and therefore consideration of our relationship with other animals is important. Animal welfare is explored. The purpose of Earth Books is to deepen our understanding of the environment and our role within it. The books featured under this imprint will both present thought-provoking questions and offer practical solutions.

If you have enjoyed this book, why not tell other readers by posting a review on your preferred book site. Recent bestsellers from Earth Books are:

In Defence of Life
Essays on a Radical Reworking of Green Wisdom
Julian Rose
Julian Rose's book has the power to lift the reader into another dimension. He offers a way to break through the destructive patterns of our consumer-obsessed society and discover a simpler, more fulfilling way forward.
Paperback: 978-1-78279-257-4 ebook: 978-1-78279-256-7

Eyes of the Wild
Journeys of Transformation with the Animal Powers
Eleanor O'Hanlon
The ancient understanding of animals as guides to self-knowledge and the soul comes alive through close encounters with some of the most magnificent creatures of the wild.
Paperback: 978-1-84694-957-9 ebook: 978-1-84694-958-6

Simplicity Made Easy
Jennifer Kavanagh
Stop wishing your life was more simple, and start making it happen! With the help of Jennifer Kavanagh's book, turn your focus to what really matters in life.
Paperback: 978-1-84694-543-4 ebook: 978-1-84694-895-4

Acorns Among the Grass
Adventures in Eco-Therapy
Caroline Brazier
When we reconnect with the natural world, we discover our deep relationship with life. This book embraces the ways in which environmental work nourishes us, psychologically and spiritually.
Paperback: 978-1-84694-619-6 ebook: 978-1-84694-883-1

Approaching Chaos
Could an Ancient Archetype Save 21st Century Civilization?
Lucy Wyatt
Civilisation can survive by learning from the social, spiritual and technological secrets of ancient civilisations such as Egypt.
Paperback: 978-1-84694-255-6

Gardening with the Moon & Stars
Elen Sentier
Organics with Ooomph! Bringing biodynamics to the ordinary
gardener.
Paperback: 978-1-78279-984-9 ebook: 978-1-78279-985-6

GreenSpirit
Path to a New Consciousness
Marian Van Eyk McCain
A collection of essays on 21st Century green spirituality and its
key role in creating a peaceful and sustainable world.
Paperback: 978-1-84694-290-7 ebook: 978-1-78099-186-3

The Protein Myth
Significantly Reducing the Risk of Cancer, Heart Disease,
Stroke, and Diabetes While Saving the Animals and Building a
Better World
David Gerow Irving
The Protein Myth powerfully illustrates how the way to vibrant
health and a peaceful world is to stop exploiting animals.
Paperback: 978-1-84694-673-8 ebook: 978-1-78099-073-6

This Is Hope
Green Vegans and the New Human Ecology: How We Find Our
Way to a Humane and Environmentally Sane Future
Will Anderson
This Is Hope compares the outcomes of two human ecologies;
one is tragic, the other full of promise...
Paperback: 978-1-78099-890-9

Safe Planet
Renewable Energy Plus Workers' Power
John Cowsill
Safe Planet lays out a roadmap of renewable energy sources and
meteorological data to direct us towards a safe planet.
Paperback: 978-1-78099-682-0 ebook: 978-1-78099-683-7

Readers of ebooks can buy or view any of these bestsellers by
clicking on the live link in the title. Most titles are published
in paperback and as an ebook. Paperbacks are available in
traditional bookshops. Both print and ebook formats are
available online.
Find more titles and sign up to our readers' newsletter at http://
www.johnhuntpublishing.com/non-fiction
Follow us on Facebook at https://www.facebook.com/
JHPNonFiction